GETTING YOUR MESSAGE ACROSS

Kurt Hanks

CRISP PUBLICATIONS

Library of Congress Cataloging-in-Publication Data

Hanks, Kurt, 1947-
    Getting your message across / Kurt Hanks, Gerreld Pulsipher.
        p.   cm.
    Includes bibliographical references.
    ISBN 1-56052-063-9 (pbk.)
    1. Communication.   I. Pulsipher, Gerreld L.   II. Title.
P90.H298 1990   90-55626
302.2—dc20   CIP

GETTING YOUR MESSAGE ACROSS

CREDITS
Contributors: **Gerreld Pulsipher,
Lisa Vermillion, Larry Belliston**
Editor: **Lisa Vermillion**
Illustrations: **Kurt Hanks**

Copyright © 1991 by Crisp Publications, Inc.
Printed in the United States of America

English language Crisp books are distributed worldwide. Our
major international distributors include:

CANADA: Reid Publishing, LTD., Box 7267, Oakville, Ontario
Canada L6J 6L6. TEL: (416) 842-4428, FAX: (416) 842-9327

AUSTRALIA: Career Builders, P. O. Box 1051, Springwood,
Brisbane, Queensland, Australia 4127. TEL: 841-1061,
FAX: 841-1580

NEW ZEALAND: Career Builders, P. O. Box 571, Manurewa,
Auckland, New Zealand. TEL: 266-5276, FAX: 266-4152

JAPAN: Phoenix Associates Co., Mizuho Bldg. 2-12-2, Kami
Osaki, Shinagawa-Ku, Tokyo 141, Japan. TEL: 443-7231,
FAX: 443-7640

Selected Crisp titles are also available in other languages.
Contact International Rights Manager Tim Polk at (415)
949-4888 for more information.

Library of Congress Catalog Card Number 90-84076
Hanks, Kurt
Getting Your Message Across
ISBN 1-56052-063-9

Contents

Contents

Contents

Contents

Contents

A reader may feel uncomfortable with my global use of the pronoun *He* throughout the book. When he/she encounters *He* when s/he thinks it should be *She* or *He/She*, she or he may remember how painful it was to read this paragraph and accept sincere apologies from this author for the frequent use of the pronoun *He*, when he really meant *He or She*.

Too often we spend our efforts on communication techniques that don't work.

The Biggest Communication Mistake

We spend most of our time communicating. But there are problems. Often, we waste our efforts on communication techniques that don't work.

- In his weekly meeting the bureaucrat asks for feedback on his memo. The unanimous response: "What memo?"

- In the hall the manager overhears two employees joking about the company newsletter: "I'd never have any trash if it weren't for that!"

- Behind his back, a teacher is called "Oliver the Ogre." His efforts at teaching are often misunderstood. When he opens his mouth, it is usually to change feet.

The biggest communication mistake is to assume that when you send a message, it has been communicated. In order to achieve communication, meaning must be transferred or exchanged. Simply speaking or writing a message does not guarantee that the message has been received—only that it has been sent.

Stiff Competition

It's getting harder and harder to communicate with workers, customers, clients, family—people in general. The sheer volume of messages bombarding every person on a daily basis has increased the chances for failure as people's attention decreases. When problems of garbled or muddied thinking or breakdowns in transmitting or receiving communication occur, people will simply turn to other messages and senders and ignore the unclear communication completely. Effective communication is absolutely critical to success.

> *The vacuum created by a failure to communicate will quickly be filled with rumor, misrepresentations, drivel, and poison.*
>
> C. Northcote Parkinson

11

Peter Drucker, speaking of the new skills needed by the manager of tomorrow (which is already here!), said, "He will have to be able to communicate information fast and clearly."

The purpose of this book is to help you identify and overcome some of the problems of communicating so that your message will be the one to which people pay attention. It is a collection of ideas on how to increase communication effectiveness.

One Idea Can Make the Difference

You'll find dozens of ideas in this book. It is hoped that at least a few ideas will be new ideas—new tips that can help with your communication problems. One tip, one slight adjustment in your communicating style, might be all you need to reap great rewards.

And what if you do find a whole bunch of communication techniques that are new to you? That doesn't mean you need to use them all, or all at once. That could be overwhelming. Then you would be worrying more about the *communication process* than about *effectively communicating*.

Instead, start small: make a little change here, a small improvement there. Then, as you feel more and more confident in the effectiveness of your communication, you can return to this book for *more* tips!

Definitions

Sometimes words change meaning as they travel from head to head—not to mention from city to city! Because of that, here are a few definitions that are crucial for us to have in common. If for some reason we're not on the same wavelength about what the words mean, this book's message will be lost.

Communication. *The process whereby one person transfers meaning to another person. Invariably, the communicator has a well-defined reason for trying to transfer the things he understands. Persuasion is often involved.*

Information. *This includes facts, figures, statistics, theories, processes, techniques, descriptions, and the like. Information has no value in and of itself, but it can assume value in certain contexts.*

Communication of Information. *The process whereby one person transfers facts, figures, etc., to another person for a well-defined reason. Whatever that reason, the underlying purpose is almost always to cause change.*

Three Steps to Effective Communication

When a person is speaking in a language his audience can't understand, an interpreter is called in. The interpreter translates the words from the foreign language into words with which the audience is familiar. Only through the interpreter can comprehension come.

An interpreter translates words and ideas into a language his audience can understand

A Process of Interpretation

The same process occurs with all communication. The interpreter (communicator) takes words and ideas with which he or she is familiar and puts them in language the audience can understand.

All communication is essentially a process of translating what the audience doesn't know into something they can know.

- **The French teacher** communicates the words and concepts of French grammar to the student. The teacher interprets the subject for the student.

- **The teacher of child psychology** translates the technical aspects of his field into languate the average mother can understand. He interprets the ideas for her.

- **The business manager** takes the critical information needed to reach the desired production levels and communicates it to subordinates.

- **Parents** take the things they understand about life and behavior and communicate them to their children. In doing so, they speak on a level the children can understand, interpreting the information for them.

• **A news commentator** analyzes the events of the day and interprets them for the viewing audience.

Every communicator acts as a translator. He takes ideas, thoughts, or information that are in one "language" he understands, and he restates them in a "language" that will be meaningful to the audience.

Everyone Interprets for Others

Whenever you communicate, you are an interpreter. You may not be interpreting a foreign language, but the subject you're communicating could well be foreign to your audience.

In interpretation, three steps invariably take place:

1. The interpreter hears or learns the ideas he plans to communicate.

2. The interpreter takes the ideas and mentally changes them into different words and images, ones his audience can understand more readily.

3. The interpreter then communicates those thoughts to his audience.

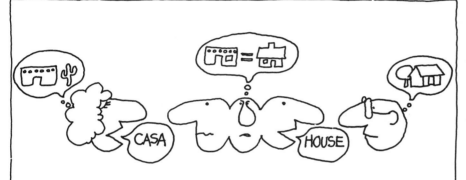

A translator hears the words spoken in one person's language, finds comparable meanings in another's language, then restates the message in an understandable manner.

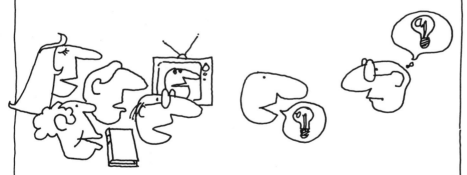

Interpretive communication is basically the same process as translating languages. You take the information from one source, find comparable meanings the audience is familiar with, then explain the information in a way the audience will understand.

Overlook This and You're Headed for Failure

All communication has a common goal: to get the audience to change. You want them to buy something they don't have, believe something they haven't believed, become something they haven't been, use something they haven't been using, understand something they haven't known, do something they haven't been doing. In a word, change.

If the audience doesn't change, there's no real reason for the communication—unless you just like to hear yourself talk. Communication without change as its prime objective is useless. It is a waste of time—though the majority of communication seems to be lacking this critical reason for its existence.

Communication Success

The degree of change thus becomes an important measure of the success of communication. The audience must change from point A to point B, from where they are to where you want them to be. They must

change their position. The change can be emotional, intellectual, physical, or a combination of all three, but it must occur for your effort to be successful.

If you're able to effect change, your communication has justification. Without it you're just blowing hot air on a windy night.

Before   After

The goal of all effective communication is to cope with change—either to avoid or cause it.

How to Organize Your Message

New information is easier to learn when it is presented according to a sequence.

To be effective, all information must follow some kind of sequence. Sometimes the sequence is critical to the information—step 2 must follow step 1. Other times the sequence is important in different ways—spacing, rhythm, contrast, interest, ease of use.

This book, for example, has a random sequence pattern. Each concept unit, which is designated by a bold head at the top of a page, can stand alone. It doesn't matter which concept unit you read first. The sequence chosen for this book takes into consideration rhythm, spacing, and ease of use after you've read the book.

Some kinds of sequences you can consider when you plan your communication are:

1. Numerical or Alphabetical   1-2-3 and a-b-c are examples of a numerical or alphabetical sequence.

2. Chronological   Before-after, history-growth, beginning-end, past-present-future. Most histories and biographies follow this kind of sequence.

3. Progressive   Simple to complex, easy to hard, familiar to strange. A good science text will follow the progressive sequence, introducing the subject in degrees until the student can understand its more complex aspects.

4. Logical   Specific to general, general to specific, inductive or deductive, cause then effect, action then reaction, need then goal, problem then implication, problem then solution.

5. Discovery   Reorder, discover here then there, hit then miss, take the information as it comes.

6. Spatial   Ocean-coast-inland, federal-state-local or metropolitan-suburban-rural, top-middle-bottom, inside-outside. Maps, travelogues, geographies, and the like follow spatial sequences. Usually art communicates spatially.

7. Topical   Who-what-when-where-why-and-how, theory-practice, flora, fauna, animal, vegetable, mineral, political, social, philosophical. Most nonfiction books follow a topical sequence, outlining their topics by subject area.

8. Motivational Gain attention, build interest, create desire, spur to action. Motivational speakers and fund-raising campaigns often use this sequence.

Right Sequence—Wrong Order

A mistake in the communication of sequence can be nothing less than disastrous. One time when many roads in Los Angeles were in dire need of repairs, government supervisors decided that the road department should fix the roads in one part of the city by:

First, digging up the road, replacing worn-out pipes, and recovering the holes;

Second, resurfacing the asphalt;

Third, painting new lines.

But when the work orders came to the road department, the sequence was confused. They explicitly instructed road workers to:

First, repaint the lines on the road;

Second, resurface the asphalt;

Third, dig up the road, replace worn-out pipes, and recover the holes.

Life Is Full of Sequences

Our lives are dominated by sequences. The heart beats in a rhythm that patterns everything we do. We eat our meals in sequence: breakfast, lunch, dinner, then back to breakfast. The food of each meal is put into a sequence: salad, soup, main course, dessert. We dress in sequence: underwear, outer clothing, socks, shoes. Dancing is a repeated pattern of sequences. Writing puts words in a grammatical sequence. Everything about us operates in sequences.

And that's how communication works best. Find the sequence that best fits the message, and you'll be amazed at how easily it is understood!

> *Instruction consists of leading the learner through a sequence of statements and restatements of a problem or body of knowledge that increases the learner's ability to grasp, transform, and transfer what he is learning.*
>
> Jerome Bruner

17

Pulling the Right Strings

Meaning is in the mind of the receiver. The goal of every communicator should be to send information or ideas in such a way as to evoke the desired meaning in the audience.

Without such a reception, the communicator's talk is only strange sounds going out across the room. His book is only weird marks on a page. His moving image is only flickering lights on a wall.

Pulling Strings to Evoke Meaning

The objective is to pull the right strings on the audience. To do that, the communicator needs to know which string is tied to which response in the audience. He needs to know how high to lift each string and how soon to let it back down again.

Communication has three objectives:

1. **To make the audience *think or know* something**
2. **To make them *feel* something**
3. **To make them *do* something**

It's essentially an effort of pulling the right strings. By saying and showing the correct things, the communicator can make the audience think. If different things are said, the audience will feel. And if they feel to the desired degree, they will do.

These three objectives are not something external to the audience; they are inside. Yet the only way to fulfill these motives is by the external manipulation of the elements of communicating that evokes a desired internal reaction—that is, by pulling strings.

String Pulling Examples

The American Cancer Society ran a TV commercial to try to get people to stop smoking. The commercial began by showing small children dressed up in their parents' clothes. The meaning was, "Children imitate their parents." The next image was a smoldering cigarette in an ashtray. That was all there was to the commercial. But the person watching it filled in the gaps and the additional meaning was evoked in the viewer's mind: "If I smoke, my children will also."

The people running the 'Clean Up America' campaign also recognized that meaning is created in the mind. Their commercial began with a camera shot of a park. Picnic tables were all set and loaded with food. In the background were sounds of people having fun playing ball and swinging on the swings. Back to the loaded picnic table—and sounds of people eating: "Pass the ketchup, please." Finally the viewer saw who was eating: a herd of pigs.

Nothing much was said. But the viewer got the meaning anyway, because the commercial had evoked it in his mind.

A book called *Nice Girls Do* effectively used the idea of pulling strings. It worked off an old cliché ("nice girls don't do that") in a way that caused a reaction in the mind. By twisting the cliché and putting a double meaning on it, the publisher was able to evoke a desired response in the reader. The book quickly became a bestseller.

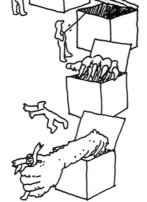

Some strings you pull may trigger something you don't want!

Trent was learning the meaning of stealing. To him, if you wanted something, you just took it. His father had tried to tell the boy about stealing—but to no avail. In frustration, he decided to join the game. "Anything of yours that I want, I will take." His father began carrying off anything of Trent's he wanted. Trent finally understood.

In all of the above examples, it was what went on in the mind of the receiver that was important. What was left unsaid may have been more important than what was said. The important thing is that the receiver got the full impact of the message.

How do you pull the right strings? Find out what is important to the audience. What are their likes, dislikes, goals, beliefs, fears, clichés? Present your message in those terms.

The American Cancer Society ad had an objective of getting people to stop smoking. But the commercial centered on the relationship between children and their parents. Often parents feel guilty when they set a bad example for their children, and they don't want to feel more guilt. The commercial exploited this fear.

People don't like to be called "pigs." What better way to cause them to clean up their act than to imply they are "pigs" if they don't? People who viewed the commercial knew exactly what was meant by calling people "pigs."

Nice girls don't, do they? You'd better pick up the book to find out.

Trent wanted possessions. Lecturing him on honesty didn't work. Turning the tables on him was a stronger way to communicate— and evoked not only meaning, but also change.

The first in a series of four critical questions about the ideas you want to get across to others.

Aside Question #1

Are you being given distorted information about your idea, thus distorting its possibilities?

Every idea is created and developed through information from various sources. This information may be about market, advertising, production, resistance, timing, costs, important people, etc., and is very important in the achievement of the results you desire. Great care should be given to insure the accuracy of this information. An error at this stage can make the success of any communication doubtful and possibly damaging.

Is your opinion valid about your idea's viability?

Do your information sources say one thing and do another?

Is there someone or something you are not listening to that is telling you critical information?

Do your sources of information have any vested interest in telling you a particular point-of-view?

Are key people telling you one thing and telling others something different?

20

Eliminate This or You'll Suffer

The more noise there is, the less communication can get through. That's pretty obvious. We've all sat through a meeting or movie with crying babies—we could hear the babies just fine, but what was being said was another matter. Even though the speaker's voice may have been loud enough for us to hear, the noise distracted us enough that we simply couldn't take it all in.

Anything in the Way

Noise is anything that gets in the way of the message. It might be actual physical noise: the crying babies or the audience talking right through the after-dinner speaker's speech. (Or, worse yet, the audience snoring through the speech!) Or it might be some other kind of distraction.

Imagine going to a theater to see a movie in a building that is old and run-down, with seats falling apart, mice running between your feet, lights burning brightly. There may be no actual noise to take you away from the movie, but there are plenty of other

kinds of noise. And every bit of it will get in the way of the communication that's being attempted.

The object is to get in control of the communication situation and reduce the noise level as much as possible. If you can control the noise, you can have much greater control over the communication that takes place. Consider the corollary to the principle stated above: The less noise there is, the greater the chance the communication will be effective.

Noise comes in many forms—and can kill communication. Here are some noises to watch out for:

- your tie is too loud
- your voice is too soft
- your voice is too raspy
- your language is too flowery
- your language is grammatically incorrect
- your written piece has typographical errors
- the setting is cluttered
- the after-dinner audience feels too sleepy
- a loud storm is going on outside

- colors in the setting clash
- it's too hot in the room
- air conditioning comes on
- people keep shifting chairs
- a wasp is buzzing in the crowd
- the audience has inadequate background on the subject
- rumor says the presentation is boring
- your name is difficult to pronounce
- the message is too long
- the message is too technical
- the paper it's printed on feels like toilet paper

A noise is anything that gets in the way of the communication. Noise is the plague of all varieties of communication: speeches, phone conversations, memos, books, slide shows, movies, magazines—everything! Noise in any form is to be scrupulously avoided!

A noise is anything that prevents the message from getting across.

Raisin Principle

When my brother was a kid he just couldn't swallow a pill. No matter what Mom tried, it just wouldn't go down. Threats of spankings or promises of candy made no difference—the pill always ended up right on the tip of his tongue. Finally Mom discovered a method that worked. She carefully cut a raisin open and inserted the pill. Then she gave it to my brother. He was able to swallow the raisin with its hidden pill, but he was never able to swallow the pill alone—even though alone it was much smaller.

Sometimes only by putting your communication within something else will you be able to get your audience to swallow it. Here are some raisins you can wrap your message in:

Raisins-Means

stories	objects	music
activities	jokes	pictures

Raisins-Media

slides	workshops	television
books	lecture	film

If your message is a bit hard to swallow, wrap it in a raisin to help it go down easier.

People would rather be entertained than educated. You may have to entertain them in order to get your message across. You may have to insert your information into something else much larger in order to have it swallowed.

This You've Got to See!

The most powerful pictures in the world are those we create in our minds.

People read faster than they can talk, and they can think even faster than that. **The only way to hold their attention is to create pictures in their minds.**

The average person talks about 100 words per minute, reads at 200 words per minute, and thinks at a rate of over 500 words per minute. So what happens when you give a talk verbally or try to communicate something in writing? The audience's minds are going at a clip that far exceeds your ability to occupy them. They start daydreaming, start thinking about things that don't fit with your communication at all. Their minds occupy themselves with something other than your message.

But what if you give them mental pictures to think about?

The more you create mental pictures in the audience's minds, the better they will see what you're trying to communicate.

Through mental pictures, the audience creates in their own minds visualizations of what you're saying. Then your message becomes more than words. It becomes mental reality. People will create far better pictures in their heads than you could ever show their eyes.

Picture This

Shep had been our dog for as long as I could remember. When I was little he licked my tears away when I was hurt; when I got older he followed me out to the barn to keep me company as I did my chores.

He was more than an animal; Shep was one of the family.

But now he was old, and he suffered more pain each day he lived. He was nearly blind, with one eye going white, and you could tell he hurt when he walked. Finally he did little more than lie by our back door, though he would follow me when I went somewhere.

Our family could see the pain in his eyes every time he moved—and it got to be too much. We knew it was time to put him out of his misery. Dad couldn't do it. "Shep's just like one of the kids," he said.

I ended up being the one to do it. I loaded the gun and climbed onto my horse. Just as always, Shep followed along, limping slightly. I rode down our dirt lane and across a wide, green meadow, then up into the foothills that flow into our town. I rode through the brush until I found a secluded place.

While still on the horse, I took aim as Shep circled a few yards away. I slowly squeezed the trigger, which seemed incredibly stiff. The gun fired with a jerk when the dog crossed in front of the horse—then suddenly the horse gave way and fell to the ground, pinning me under him. I had shot my horse in the neck!

The walk back home was more painful for me than it ever was for old Shep, who followed faithfully along behind.

Create Images in Their Heads

Mental pictures are so powerful that I'm sure you saw many of the things that happened in that story. Yet what you saw was individual to you—and thus was even more powerful. The dog you saw was differ-

ent from the dog I saw in the story; the horse was different; the meadow and the hills were different. We both created images of what happened, and that's what makes any communication effective. We imagine in our heads a more complete picture than words alone could ever create.

Alfred Hitchcock was a master at showing horror. But the genius in what he did was in what he didn't show.

Through suggestion he created images in our minds, so we saw things that weren't really there. He would begin the image, and our minds completed it, making his stories much more frightening than they would have been if he had simply shown us everything. His objective, as he stated it, was to "transfer the menace on the screen to the minds of the audience."

If you can create pictures in the minds of your audience, the communication is more likely to be effective.

The second in a series of four critical questions about the ideas you want to get across to others.

Aside Question #2

Are you trying to get your idea across to the wrong audience?

You may waste a considerable amount of resources (such as, time, money, and effort) by talking to the wrong audience. You may even hinder the response you desire with your real intended audience. The greatest return on any time you may spend in communicating is the time you take identifying, defining, targeting, and testing your intended audience. Their response to your ideas' success is the reason for communicating in the first place.

Will they value your idea?

Do they have the capacity to understand your idea?

Do they have the capacity to expedite your idea in the way you desire, if they accept it?

Will their ego or existing paradigm prevent them from accepting your ideas?

Could acceptance of your idea by this audience hurt you in any way?

How to Make a Message Simple to Understand

Tongue

Stomach

Intestines

Man

Gastro-intestinal tract—unraveled.

People learn easiest when the new thing they are being taught relates to things already known.

It's very difficult, if not impossible, to learn something totally new. **People learn easiest when the new thing they are being taught relates to things already known.**

Knowing this is critical to communication. The communicator can be much more effective if he relates the information to things the audience has already experienced. This approach is called apperception.

Apperception (ap-er-sep-shun) n., the process of understanding something perceived in terms of previous experience.

A person can't understand what he can't relate to. But using the approach of apperception puts your message on a level that the audience can understand.

The Apperceptive Approach

Look how the following facts come into perspective when we use apperception:

Fact A grasshopper can jump twenty times the length of its body.
Apperception Approach If you could jump that well you could span a football field in three leaps.

Fact The diameter of an atom is about one-hundredth of a millionth of an inch.
Apperception Approach That means if you were to enlarge an orange to the size of the earth, the atoms that make up the orange would be the size of cherries. Then to see the nucleus of each atom, you must further enlarge the cherry-size atoms to be as big as the Houston Astrodome. The nucleus would then be the size of a grain of salt.

27

Fact There are 100 billion stars in our galaxy.
Apperception Approach If every star in our galaxy were a grain of rice, it would take forty railroad cars to hold them.

Fact You need to be careful if you sneeze while you're driving, since your eyes will automatically close.
Apperception Approach If you sneeze while driving at 55 miles per hour, you'll travel 250 yards with your eyes closed.

Fact We use a lot of water in America.
Apperception Approach One flush of the toilet uses up more water in five seconds than an average family in Africa uses in one day.

Fact: Tyrannosauruses were carnivorous. Apperception Approach: they would have eaten men—if there had been any!

Fact Flies have a lot of offspring.
Apperception Approach If you got one male and one female housefly together in April and let them breed, outlawing fly swatters and poisons, their offspring would cover the entire face of the earth to a depth of one inch by fall.

Fact Clocks are turned ahead one hour the first Sunday in April and are turned back an hour the last Sunday in October.
Apperception Approach Spring forward, fall back.

Fact Atoms are mostly filled with empty space.
Apperception Approach The proportion of the distances between particles in an atom is the same proportion as the distances between planets in our solar system.

One Thing to Remember

In most communication situations, people find themselves either without anything to say or with too much to say and not enough time. If you don't have anything to say, neither this nor any other book will help. But if you have too much to say in the allotted time, that's where this book can help. When that time comes, you'll have a choice of two courses: The Hard Line, or the Bland Compromise.

The Hard Line takes a serious look at what you have to say and pares down the nonessentials. It takes those six main points you've worked up and cuts them down to one important concept. It's better to explain one idea well than to cover several poorly.

The Bland Compromise tries to squeeze everything in. Shift this and juggle that and hope it will work—though it rarely does. This approach will end up lacking strength or power. It will end up bland.

Too many communicators spend too much time and energy trying to be all things to all people. Like the politician who tries to

Everyone is pointing a different way, trying to be all things to all people. They're going to end up being nothing.

please everyone, these communicators will end up being nothing, having nothing, and accomplishing nothing at all.

Taking the Hard Line and concentrating on only the most important objectives is nearly always more effective.

Big Bland Book for the Boys in Business

One college-level business textbook presently on the market was created by a committee. It's not a good book, and it's no surprise that it's not selling well, even though it cost almost half a million dollars to produce. The text was created by compromise. One committee member said, "I want this." Another said, "I want that." A third said, "I want this." And so on. . . .

Rather than limiting what the book should include, the committee decided to incorporate all the ideas. They ended up with a 600-page bland book. The only thing a reader can get from it is a hernia.

Compromising with Elephants

Most compromises end up creating more problems than they solve. It's like trying to stop a charging elephant with shotguns, BB guns, and pellet guns. Even if you manage to hit him with all those separate little pellets, he won't stop. He'll just get madder. Both you and your gun will be stomped into the ground by one angry animal. None of those small pellets will ever get through his thick hide. Only a lot of power moving a single bullet toward one critical point will work.

You are not shooting elephants; you are trying to communicate. But the situation is similar:

• You can't afford a mad audience charging at you.

• Your communication must get through.

• You must cause them to have a specific reaction.

• You've got to penetrate their thick hides.

He who tries to be all things to all people ends up being nothing to everybody.

Quick Fix Failure

The basic principles of communication are relatively easy to list. They're easy to understand, once you take the time. But application is another matter. Successful communication is seldom easy. It always takes time and effort and understanding.

A quick fix won't bring success when it comes to communication. There are no shortcuts or easy ways out. The only approach that works is the one that comes with applied effort. Sir Laurence Olivier was once interviewed about the magic he created on the stage. Olivier replied, "Listen, the magic is in the audience. What is on the stage is hard work."

Every day we turn on our television sets and see hundreds of attempts at communication. Some are more successful than others, but every one has taken hours and hours of planning and lots of bucks. A successful commercial, for example, will take six months to produce, will cost over $500,000, and will run only thirty seconds. The producers can't schlock the commercial together just because the message is short.

Shortcuts to effective communication may take you where you don't want to go.

They have to pay the price and spend the needed time on it. They know that quick fixes don't do the trick.

You learn to read by reading. And you learn to communicate by communicating. There are no easy answers to communication. Everyone has to learn by doing it.

The Biggest Problem Is Three Problems

Making communication work involves solving three problems, not just one.

The biggest problem with creating effective communication is that people treat communicating as one big problem. But it's not. Being able to communicate effectively involves overcoming three problems. They are very separate challenges and require different skills.

Getting TO the people.
This is a technical problem. To resolve it, the communicator must reach his audience, attract them to his ideas. He has to get the people and the ideas together.

Getting INTO the people.
This is a perceptual problem. The communicator considers how he can get the audience involved in what he has to tell them, and how to get them to assimilate the information once he gives it.

Getting a response OUT of the people.
This is an obtaining-results problem. The communicator has the challenge of getting the audience to retain what he says—and then to apply it.

Making communication work involves solving three problems, not just one.

One Big Problem—One Big Flop

When a person treats these separate problems as one, he often ends up with complete failure. Each problem involves different approaches using different tools and different skills.

- I know of a warehouse full of 100,000 copies of a certain book that never sells. The book is very well done. But nobody knows about it. The problem of getting it TO the people was never solved.

- I know of a seminar program that helps people fall asleep, though that was never its motive. The information presented at the seminar is very useful and could be very valuable to people attending the seminar. But it is presented in a very uninteresting way. The problem of getting it INTO the people was never solved.

•I know of a public service agency that was up to its neck in trouble from an outraged public when the public mistook what its commercials were saying for a threat. The problem of getting the right response OUT of the people was never solved.

To be successful, communication must solve each of these three problems.

It's not enough to get the communication TO the people. It must also get INTO them. Then the communicator must get the right response OUT of them.

The third in a series of four critical questions about the ideas you want to get across to others.

Aside Question #3

What if you got your idea across and caught more than you bargained for?

Often we see only the side of our communication success that is benefical, but there may be negative side effects related to getting what we wanted. Our resources can be severely taxed, especially if you must become the champion of the idea and must see it through all stages of its growth and application. Some ideas, once they get started, have a life of their own and they demand constant feeding and attention.

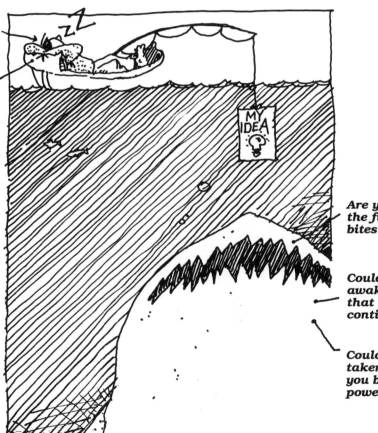

Are you asleep to factors that you are not now anticipating?

Do you really want to catch what you're fishing for? Are you committed to reeling it in?

Are you ready for the future if it bites?

Could your idea awaken a monster that must be continually fed?

Could your idea be taken away from you by more powerful forces?

34

Different Modes for Different Folks

Everyone learns differently. Match your style to your mode of learning, and everything will become easier.

Tasting   **Touching**   **Seeing**   **Hearing**   **Smelling**

Different people think in different ways. They have to tailor-fit their communication to themselves. The approach has to change to fit precisely with each communicator.

There are many different ways to communicate. Sometimes you won't have a choice as to which approach you use—but if you have a choice, for heaven's sake, make sure you fit it to your own personality.

Some people are better at writing. Some communicate best through speaking. Some are more visual or even more tactile.

Using the Wrong Mode of Expression

One expert knew his field thoroughly. He knew he could make a great contribution if he published a book. But he was a lousy writer; he just couldn't get the feel of the written word. He tried for years to produce a book, but he couldn't pull it off. Finally he realized he should fit his communication to his personality. The expert could talk about his subject anytime—so he talked the book

into a tape recorder. Finally he was able to complete the work!

The more your method and style of communicating match your mode of thinking, the more strength there will be in your communication. Your communication must fit with who you are. It needs to work in harmony with your natural style and skills.

Show and Tell

One of my kids had to give a talk to a group of other kids. He couldn't read very well—but he was visually oriented. So I helped him fit the communication to himself. Instead of speaking from notes, he spoke from little pictures he'd drawn. It made all the difference to him. By making things fit he was able to free his thinking and communicate effectively.

Mark Twain is a good example of fitting your communication to yourself. Twain was an excellent writer—one of the greatest America has ever produced. But when he started on the lecture circuit, he discovered that writing and speaking are two different processes.

He tried memorizing the first letter of key sentences, as well as the sentence itself. To assure himself that he'd remember, he wrote the letters on his fingernails. But it was hard to keep track of the fingers. "I was never quite sure which finger I'd used last," he wrote later.

Then he struck on an idea that worked for him! He realized that it's hard to visualize letters and words and sentences—but it's easy to visualize and remember pictures. "In two minutes I made six pictures with a pen," he wrote, "and they did the work of eleven catch-sentences, and did it perfectly."

Find What Works for You

Once Twain found the approach to communication that fit him, he was able to give the kind of speeches he had always dreamed of. Drawing pictures may not be the key for all of us, but aligning who you are and how you work to how you're communicating is a key that can make all kinds of difference in the effectiveness of your presentation.

Order Existing Knowledge

People are constantly being deluged by information. Voices are all around us, incessantly demanding our attention, trying to tell us the new and the different. The need isn't for the new. Most of us already have far more information than we know what to do with. What we do need— desperately—is for someone to help us understand and order what we already know.

Much of the work of the communicator is to give order to knowledge that's already in the heads of the audience. The communicator's purpose is giving meaning to things people are already familiar with.

Give Order to What They Already Have

Instead of trying to cram new information into someone's head, give order to knowledge a person already has. The audience already has plenty of information in their minds. The communicator can put that information into patterns they've never seen before.

We already have too much information to know what to do with.

The whole key to communication is understanding what the audience already has in their minds and then helping them put it into new order.

- Take random knowledge in the mind
- Show how the pattern fits together
- It becomes a new pattern in the mind

The surest way to impress someone is to tell him the meaning of the facts he already knows.

George V. Higgins

Provide a Structure for Understanding

Transactional analysis serves as a good example of how information can be ordered in a new way. TA puts all of us in one of three categories: adult, parent, and child.

Parent Ego State		
Adult Ego State	P	P
	A	A
Child Ego State	C	C
	One person's relationship to another	

Everyone can relate to those titles; everyone knows what an adult or parent or child is. In helping us to see those relationships in a new way, Transactional Analysis has made a meaningful contribution.

Another example is the popular misspelling dictionary. Its editors took the most commonly misspelled words and made a dictionary out of them—spelling them the wrong way! The regular dictionary wasn't helping misspellers—if a person knew enough about the correct spelling to look the word up, he probably didn't need the dictionary. But with the misspeller's dictionary, the person would be able to find the word he needed and learn how to spell it correctly.

The misspelling dictionary doesn't tell the user anything new. It doesn't contain entries or definitions that are different from the ordinary dictionary. All it does is take existing knowledge and put it in a new order.

Better Use of What They Know

You cannot teach a man anything. You can only help him to discover it within himself.

Galileo

Communication is a process of causing meaning in the receiver's mind. Most communication specializes in the transfer of new information or new knowledge. But that's putting the emphasis in the wrong place. Communicators who will help us organize and use the information that we've already received are much more needed.

Any audience brings many times more information to the communication setting than the communicator could ever put in. The problem is not so much in putting it across as in getting it out.

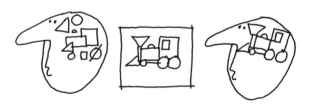

Take random knowledge in the mind,

Show how the pattern fits together,

It becomes a new pattern in the mind.

The whole key to communication is understanding what the audience already has in their minds and then helping them put it into new order.

K.I.S.S.

Two salesmen, according to an old story (which just has to be true!), were discussing ways to reach their prospects effectively.

"I lay it all out for them," said the first. "I bombard them with so many facts and figures that they could never say 'no' to me."

"Not me," said the second. "I just kiss them, and they melt into my arms every time. That's why I'm able to lead the company year after year."

Well, the first salesman started to think about his friend's approach. "Maybe it will work," he thought to himself. "Besides, it sounds fun."

At his first call of the day, a beautiful woman answered the door. Without saying a word, the salesman grabbed her and gave her a big kiss. Taken aback, the woman did nothing at first; but when she got her wits about her, she pushed the man back, slapped him, and slammed the door

Keep **I**t **S**imple, **S**tupid!

in his face. "It didn't work quite right," he told himself as he walked to his next door. "But I'm green at this approach. And it sure is fun."

He rang the doorbell and waited, his lips puckered and waiting. A shriveled old man shuffled to the door and opened it.

spot. "I'll bombard him with facts and figures."

K.I.S.S. Keep it simple, stupid. It is bluntly stated, rarely understood, and often forgotten. It's an old approach to communication, but no less effective for that. The more complex your communication gets, the less effective it is.

Complex communication is:

• harder for the audience to fit together into a pattern;

• harder for the audience to remember;

• harder for the audience to understand.

In communicating we tend to tell it all. We want to tell the audience everything we know about a subject. But the more we say, the less they understand. The material might be old hat to us—but it's new to the audience, and they can't handle it all.

A good presentation is usually one with a single concept, organized in a straightforward manner, and presented in a highly illustrated way.

One of my friends once took his family Christmas shopping—and his mother-in-law went along. The mother-in-law had a tendency to be a back-seat driver, and she was in fine form that evening. Every little move my friend made would elicit a whoop or a holler or a quick order from his mother-in-law. It didn't take long for him to overload; the situation was just too complex. Add the mother-in-law to the flashing traffic lights to the fighting kids next to him—and my friend hit another car. He wasn't a bad or careless driver. He was just the victim of too much input from too many sources.

Simple Is Better

A successful university football coach who uses no more than a dozen plays said, "A simple play, executed well, with precision and speed, is more likely to move the ball and gain the needed yardage than a detailed and complicated one." Simplicity is a key in his team's game playing. A communicator also has to move the ball into his receiver's hands. But with complexity causing poorly run plays, the ball is often dropped.

In essence, "Keep It Simple, Stupid."

If you want an example of how to keep your communication simple, compare Lincoln's Gettysburg address to the latest bill from Congress. One of them says it all very simply and briefly, yet beautifully. The other talks a lot but says very little.

Everything should be made as simple as possible, but not simpler.

Albert Einstein

Short words are best and the old words, when short, are best of all.

Winston Churchill

Think as wise men do, but speak as the common people do.

Aristotle

Communication That Attracts

Sometimes buildings grow up topsy-turvy—a conglomeration of forms and functions. I can think of one particular building like that. On one corner is a taco joint. On the other side is a sign advertising an accounting firm. Up on the second floor is a clothing warehouse. One part of the architecture is modern; another part is early American; another part is classical shack. What goes on inside has no relationship to the outside and vice versa.

Such a building is an eyesore. It does nothing well. It repels rather than attracts. People would rather avoid it than approach it. They can't define what it is or what it does.

The Communication Lacks Structure

Some communication turns out like the eyesore building. The speaker or writer can't seem to decide whether he's telling an extended joke, presenting an essay, or pitching an advertisement. He jumps from a critical point to a far-out anecdote. He leaps to his mother's favorite song, then to another critical point—but this point is on another topic!

Information that's communicated well is unified and attractive; it has a stable and cohesive structure.

Communication might be very memorable in its parts and still be ineffective. The audience might laugh at all the jokes. They may nod in agreement at the points made. But if the communication isn't well structured, it won't accomplish its purpose. It will be remembered for all the wrong reasons. And it certainly won't motivate an audience to action.

Building Codes

Creating good communication is very much like designing a building. Coordinating styles and elements must be used throughout. Though it be solid gold and the finest workmanship, early American decor does not fit well with most modern architecture. And communication works the same way. The parts must blend with the structure to make a cohesive message.

• **Communicate Only One Idea.** Find your central point and stick to it. A building has to have a good foundation—only one foundation!—and communication is just the same.

• **Avoid Weak Elements.** Weak elements are most often stories, jokes, and examples. Don't misunderstand—those are vital elements much of the time. But unless they clarify or support the main idea, they become weak elements that can collapse the entire structure.

• **Avoid Disjointed, Poorly Connected Elements.** Poorly connected plumbing pipes in a building will leak water. Poorly connected building elements could collapse the whole building. Communicators

often know what they mean, but fail in communicating the relevance to an audience. A point that seems to have come from left field may be vital to the main message, but unless the communicator helps make the connection, it may go unseen by the audience.

The Optimum Structure

You know your communication is a stable and unified structure when you can't add something or take it away without damaging the whole thing.

. . . unless detail is placed into a structured pattern, it is rapidly forgotten.

Jerome Bruner

Making Your Audience Want to Listen

Never judge a warrior until you've walked a mile in his moccasins.

Old Indian saying

The more you can understand an audience and see things from their point of view, the better your chances of reaching them in a meaningful way.

Each person in the audience has his own hang-ups, concerns, and preoccupations. If you try to approach that person from your viewpoint, you'll probably fail to reach him.

Darlene, a financial counselor, showed up in our office one day. She was excited about some information we had prepared about earning additional income. "This material teaches the same principles that I use in financial counseling," she said. "But instead of telling people *how to budget money,* you tell them *how to put an extra $100 in your pocket.* The information is basically the same, but your approach sounds more interesting to them. People want to hear what you have to say more than they want to hear what I have to say."

Sometimes, this may seem like the only way to achieve a "captive" audience.

Darlene was telling people what she thought they should hear. She was telling them what she wanted them to hear. But they were only interested in what they wanted to hear.

The secret is to tell people what you want to tell them—but tell it in terms of what they want to hear.

See a situation through the audience's eyes. Empathize with their emotions. Get into their minds so you can experience things as they do, using their filter to perceive things. Compare your objectives, symbols, information, and language with the audience's. And if they don't match, don't waste your time trying to change the audience, at least not on that level. Instead, approach them on their own ground, and deliver your message from that point.

The Empathy Meter

One way that may be helpful is to test your communication with an imaginary empathy meter. The meter has several broad measuring points, each indicating audience reaction. The points are hate, dislike, boredom, like, and love. Consider your communication from the audience's point of view, measure what you want to say against their anticipated reaction. If they don't like or love it, you're not doing well with empathy. Make the necessary changes so that the needle will move in the right direction across the meter.

Hate	Dislike	Bored	Like	Love

How does the audience react to various parts of your communication?

Use your imagination to listen through the ears of the audience and see through their eyes. Will the audience like, dislike, or be bored with the message? Or will they thoroughly despise what they hear? Let the meter tell you.

I Love You

The need for empathy can extend even as far as the actual words used. For example, Mary came from a family whose parents rewarded acceptable behavior with love.

Whenever Mary did something that pleased her parents, they would show and speak of their love for her. But only then. "I love you" was said only when she did the right things.

Ralph came from a family where love was unconditional. Even when Ralph did something that displeased his parents, they loved him and told him so. His parents expressed love independently of Ralph's actions.

When Ralph and Mary got married, they had a few difficulties in their communication. They'd often tell each other "I love you"—but it meant different things to each of them. Without good empathy for each other, they were speaking two different languages.

A communicator can be in the same fix. Real empathy has to stem from the very roots of a person's motivations and behavior. The sensitive communicator can feel how an audience is responding and adjust the message accordingly.

Empathy is the best way to reach an audience.

A Sure Test for Success

Once upon a time . . .

A wise old owl: *What did you want your communication project to accomplish?*

A proud peacock: *To get across the image that this company is really great.*

Owl: *Did you get that image across?*

Peacock: *Sure did! I told them all about the company and they got the picture.*

Owl: *When they saw how neat the company was, what did they do?*

Peacock: *Well, of course, they felt the company was a fantastic place. But I don't see why I have to stand here and answer these very obvious questions. It was my project— my baby. I spent the money carefully and did the job that had to be done.*

Owl: *Can I ask just one more?*

Peacock: *Okay. . . . Make it short.*

Don't be fooled by the proud peacock—he is all talk but no real results.

Owl: *What exactly would give me any indication from your audience that you succeeded?*

Peacock: *Well, they would . . . ah . . . oh, you could . . . maybe . . . er . . . ah . . . just because they did.*

It is easy for someone to spout off—to say what they want to say. The proud peacock

45

is like a lot of other birds who like to hear themselves talk. They think others are listening, but they never check to find out for sure. And that's okay, sometimes. But if you want to communicate with someone, you have to be sure they got the message. And the way to do that is to observe their reactions. If they didn't get the message, or didn't care about the message, nothing will happen.

If you bought this book, it was because you want your message to get across. But how many situations have you encountered where people are unwilling to check to see if their message is getting across—company newsletters, boring speeches, dull instructional movies, worthless books? It is way past time that the cry go out to "Prove it!"

• Prove that the communication worked!

• Prove that there are some concrete results for the effort!

• Prove that the purpose for the communication has been met!

Hold Accountable

Annually, millions upon millions of dollars are wasted, hours upon hours are lost, and the talents of a lot of good people are misused. Why? Because the person in charge of communicating is not held accountable for his or her choices. If results are what is desired, then accountability for communicating must be required.

Successful communication can only be based on having clear objectives of what the audience is expected to do—then, after the communication is finished, checking to see if they did it.

The objectives must be specific and well understood. The clearer the objectives, the easier it is to know when they've been met.

Take this book, for example. You bought it because you thought it was going to give you something you wanted. If it doesn't, you won't recommend it to anyone else. Sales will eventually fall. And we will have failed. Worse yet, you will have wasted your money. (For both our sakes, let's hope that isn't the case.)

The key to proving successful communication is to have the audience do something. Have them participate in some kind of behavior that's observable. When you have some observable behavior as your objective, you will know by the audience's actions whether or not they are responding to your message.

The communication effort will be more effective if you put objectives in writing. Do you want your audience to clap, cry, sing, buy something, come back, change old habits, or just sit there? State the objective in terms of the desired response.

If you are working with more than one person in preparing a communication piece, make sure all involved have a copy of the objectives and clearly understand them. The objectives are the criteria for all judgments of how well the communication works.

Success Is in the Results

For example, suppose you are assigned to go after some donation money. The objective isn't to spend so many hours on the job or to send out so many letters or to knock on so many doors. Your judgment of how well you've done is based on audience response—how much money they give you.

Knowing that, structure your communication accordingly. You make the presentation with your end objective in mind. And then you judge yourself on the audience's observable action: they give you the money. If you receive little or no money, you've failed. If you receive the needed donations, you've succeeded.

Who Are You Fooling?

Most communicators think they're defining their purpose, but it's only an illusion. They think the communication is working, but it's only the appearance that works.

Have you ever had anything like this happen? The manager of a company proudly shows you his new brochure. It looks nice. It looks terrific. But then comes the kicker: How well did it accomplish its objective? Did it increase sales? The answer: "We don't know for sure. How do you assign a value to a brochure like this? All indications are that it will benefit us. But we don't have any way to know for sure. It's a nice brochure, though, isn't it?" Who is that manager fooling? He is communicating to himself. He gave himself the nice brochure that he's wanted for a long time. He's only putting on the appearance of communicating.

An Objective List

This list will show the difference between a vague objective and one a lot clearer—one that you can get feedback on.

Valid Communication

To be effective, communication must have a purpose behind it. An inseparable part of that purpose is clear evidence, when finished, that the purpose was met. Why else communicate?

The clearer and simpler that objective is, the easier to see when the results are reached. A lot of speeches, slide programs, and heart-to-heart talks fail because they lack a simple direction towards accountability—proof that they work!

Vague Objectives:

- *Understand reasons for the Civil War*
- *Appreciate music*
- *Develop an awareness of creative potential*
- *Believe in conservation*
- *Support the agency*
- *Write a needed book*
- *Feel good about it*
- *Use the machine correctly*

Clear Objectives:

- *List three reasons the Civil War started*
- *Name favorite classical music selection*
- *Solve a list of problems by using unusual solutions*
- *Turn in old newspapers for recycling*
- *Talk positively about the agency*
- *Sell 1,000,000 copies*
- *Have smiles on their faces*
- *No accidents, breakdowns, or waste*

The last in a series of four critical questions about the ideas you want to get across to others.

Aside Question #4

Could someone else communicate your idea better than you?

The idea is your baby, but should you be the one that promotes its virtues? It is a common assumption that the one with the idea is the best one to communicate it, but that may not be true. The one with the skills to come up with the idea may not be the one with the skills to communicate it. The two tasks may involve different, even incompatible skills. Perhaps you should be looking for a skilled communicator to deliver your idea.

Can the person who tells of your idea understand it, or must you always be there for the needed background?

How relevant is the truth in communicating your idea?

Do they know what they are doing?

Can you get them to do what needs to be done? Could they wander off into territory you would rather they avoid?

Can your communicator be trusted with the idea? Could they run off with it and call it their own?

Is your communicator credible and believable?

Getting Others to Take Notice

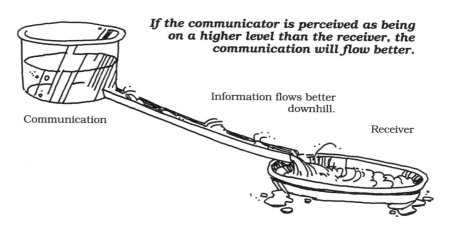

If the communicator is perceived as being on a higher level than the receiver, the communication will flow better.

Communication

Information flows better downhill.

Receiver

How much do you listen to someone you consider a dull-witted nincompoop?

Communication is like water: if it can flow downhill, things will progress much more efficiently. If the communicator is viewed as being on a higher plane than the receivers, he can send down his messages from above. And the messages will be well received. But if the communicator doesn't have a great deal of credibility, the audience may well think they know more than he does. He'll have to pump his message uphill, requiring a lot more energy and effort.

The more the audience views you as a credible source of information, the more likely the communication will have an impact on them.

In general, a suit and tie will give the communicator more credibility. But at a meeting of Nudists International, suits are out of place. Ties are optional.

A study at New York University has shown that talking faster increases credibility and audiences learn more in the process. The study also found that speeded-up commercials were remembered 36 percent more accurately than were slower ones.

Increase Your Perceived Worth

There is the old but true principle that credibility is a belief. It is an image of worth only within your audience's mind. That image is critical. It determines how the audience feels about you and your message. Everything possible should be done to upgrade your image, to increase the amount of credibility you have.

Professor of Fluff

A professor at a California university recently did an experiment to determine how important to communication credibility really is. He hired an actor to pose as a noted (but really nonexistent) psychologist and speak at a professional gathering at the university. The professor worked up some false credentials for his actor friend, including a Ph.D. and a number of published works. Then he developed a stunningly impressive talk for the actor to give, one that sounded great but was utterly devoid of meaning.

Finally the time of the seminar came. The professor's peers and working psychologists from all around came to attend. The actor appeared at the podium and performed brilliantly. Afterwards, true professionals flocked around the actor. "That was a fantastic presentation," they said.

"You just gave the best lecture I've ever heard on the subject."

"Your conclusions agreed with much that I have been researching privately."

Remember that the professor carefully engineered the talk so it would have no real content. Remember that the actor had no credentials other than the ones the professor made up for him. Despite those drawbacks, however, he had great credibility in the minds of those who listened to him. And because of that credibility, established and competent professionals sat in awe at the feet of an upstart imposter.

Picking Up a Picasso

There is a story about a man who approached the famous Picasso at a cafe. The man talked on and on about the painter's great work and said, "Here is a signed check for $10,000 for some of your artwork." Picasso grabbed the check, drew a rough sketch on the check's back and signed it. "When I cash the check you'll receive the art," Picasso then replied. The man thanked him repeatedly and walked away happily.

What happened in that man's mind to make a painter's doodle worth $10,000?

All This and More on One Sheet of Paper

A good friend of mine, whom I had worked with for years, came into the office very excited one day. He had just come back from a conference and was raving about one highly credible expert's approach to creativity. "It's an approach that always works," he said. "It will work in any organization or company. And it will work with anybody from little kids to senior citizens." He then handed me a piece of paper 8 1/2" x 11" which he claimed contained the entire fantastic method.

I proceeded to read the paper. He was still raving and waving another copy at others in the office. I finished . . . but I didn't understand it. I read the paper again—still nothing. I reread it another time. "My head must be full of mud not to grasp the importance of these ideas," I thought. Finally, one last time, I read it again, slowly and carefully.

When I took all the rhetoric, jargon, buzzwords, and generalities out of the paper, I had little left. All I had were two ands, five periods, and a comma. There honestly was nothing there! But to my friend, everything was there.

The power of credibility is one of the greatest forces in communication. The communicator spends his time well who spends it in increasing his image in the minds of those he's talking to. Sad but true: Sometimes confusion, complexity, and a few letters after your name will do a lot to increase your credibility.

Strengthening Your Presentation

The more the elements in a presentation are unified toward a single thrust, the stronger the communication will be.

Any element will lack strong meaning unless it's placed in a cohesive pattern.

Communication is composed on many levels of meaning, and each level may have many elements. The more each level is cohesive in its meaning, the more impact the overall communication will have.

Each part of the communication must be controlled so it works in harmony with the others. No element can be considered too unimportant to be carefully worked into the overall thread of the communication.

Cohesive Herbs, Unified Forest Fires

I once helped design the cover of a book on herbs. We wanted to make sure that the whole cover worked well as an overall unit. That meant that each element on the cover had to be carefully chosen. Here's what we came up with and why:

Key words:
Little
Herb
Encyclopedia

Simple design makes it look easy to read and use.

Conservative border

Traditional type style

organic lines

natural colors: soft green and brown

On another occasion I was hired to communicate through exhibits in a visitors' center the idea of preventing forest fires. Just to illustrate how important it is that the entire communication work well as a unit, let me describe one room in that center. Our purpose was to show the destructiveness of fire. Here are the elements we used:

• To make the visitor feel ill at ease, we designed the floor to appear unstable. They walked very gingerly across it.

• The room was filled with the smell of burnt trees. The low flicker of a red light illuminated the room. The central display in the room was a grouping of real burnt trees, killed in a forest fire.

• There were also many small panels that briefly explained the destructive results of forest fires.

When visitors walked into the room they would suddenly become very quiet. They stared for a moment at the trees, quickly read the panels, and then left. They didn't like the room—it was too effective. Few of them could easily forget their experience in that room. It accomplished its purpose, because every element was carefully chosen and arranged to communicate one central idea.

The Continuity of the Whole

A film is made up of separate shots and separate scenes tied together by a cohesive story line. The viewer never sees the separate shots. All he sees is the overall effect of the communication. In the language of the filmmaker, this is called continuity.

Never forget the importance of the whole in communication. In the end, that's all the audience receives. Sure, any communication is a creation of many separate elements. Communication may come in units of pages, words, gestures, shots. But these separate elements must come together in one cohesive whole if the communication is to work. If the many small things work, and if they work together, the big things will come together naturally.

A Rule for Successful Communication

Make the information accessible and easy! It is surprising how often the key information is made very hard to access.

I once had a secretary who was extremely effective. Whatever she did for us, she did very well. But then she left to get married. Oh-oh. I still can't find many of the things she filed with her own unique system.

I had thought she was the ideal secretary. But she forgot a basic rule of dealing with information: If you can't get at it, you'll never be able to use it. She could get at it but nobody else could.

Accessibility is crucial to any kind of communication. Accessibility means being able to get at something.

Packaged My Way

New ideas are usually packaged "my way." This often means that the communicator devises a new elaborate reference system. With a new system, the user has to figure out the system before he can get at the information. This approach doesn't work well. It makes the information less accessible even though the intent of the communicator is to make it more accessible.

I know of a college professor who worked for two years just on the contents arrangement of a book. The arrangement was very elaborate. But all his effort was lost on the kids who finally read it. In his desire to create a work of genius, the professor had written a book that was inaccessible to the user.

Compare that kind of book with a dictionary. You can get right into it and right out again. It is arranged so you can easily find whatever you want to find.

If information is organized according to a structure that the user can easily understand, then it is more likely the information will be used. The dictionary organizes information according to the alphabet, something everybody is familiar with.

In Order of the Most Memorable

Your friend goes to a movie or reads a novel he loves. Ask him to describe it. Chances are he'll get things out of order, telling you first about the things that had the greatest impact on him. Why? Because that's how

53

his brain provides him access to it. He recalls scenes in the movie—stand-alone units of information—not in the order they appeared in the movie, but according to how they pop into his mind. This book is organized in such a way that you can recall units of information. Each unit of information is packaged for easy use and recall. Each unit stands alone.

Packaged for Easy Access

Newsletters are examples of information packaged for easy access. People are willing to pay high prices to get accessible information. One of the most successful financial newsletters in the world, Blue Chip Economics Indicators, is based on the idea of accessibility. It is nothing fancy, not slick and polished like some newsletters. The newsletter, a monthly, is only eight pages long and is held together with a staple. But most of the nation's leading economists subscribe at a rate of $222 a year.

Why do they pay that kind of money for only 96 sheets of paper a year? The answer lies in accessibility. The newsletter is easy to get into and out of; the reader is able to easily get pertinent financial information without wading through volumes of research and data.

There is a new kind of audience out there. Two generations of television watching and the volume of information available have left an impact. The key to successful communication is to give the audience accessible information. Package the information in tight units so the receiver can get in and out of the information quickly. Package the information using more than just words—use sounds, visuals, etc.—whatever is necessary to make the information more accessible.

A Magic Formula

Surprise and humor can work magic with an audience.

Communication works a little better if it contains a touch of magic. What is magic? It's much more than card tricks and pulling rabbits out of hats. It's the ability to charm and surprise an audience while at the same time getting the message across.

Tapping into the Audience's Imagination

Magic uses the audience's imagination. Through it the communicator can take a mundane subject and end up entrancing the audience. The imagination has a great deal of depth. It is constantly filled with mystical, magical dreams and daydreams, thoughts and visions, hopes and fantasies. By tapping into that valuable source, the communicator can give a great deal of life to any presentation. Magic can come from humor, from charm, from the unexpected. As you weave some into your communication, you'll weave your audience around your fingers.

"The content of the surprise can be as various as the enterprises in which men are engaged. It may express itself in one's dealing with children, in making love, in carrying on a business, in formulating physical theory, in painting a picture. . . . Surprise is not easily defined. It is the unexpected that strikes out with wonder and astonishment. What is curious about effective surprise is that it need not be rare or infrequent or bizarre and is often none of these things. Effective surprise . . . seems rather to have the quality of obviousness about it when it occurs, producing a shock of recognition following which there is no longer astonishment. . . . The triumph of effective surprise is that it takes on beyond common ways of experiencing the world."

Jerome Bruner

Double Meaning

I once helped prepare a talk that the speaker brought off with a good deal of magic. He was trying to convey the idea that we need to build bridges between what we are and what we can be. He had projected behind him on a screen a large image of a bridge—but the entire center section was missing. He elaborated on the idea of bridges, and then brought out a visual aid.

He had a young man and a young woman come out. They were dirty and scruffy; their hair was unkempt and their clothes were sloppy. They slouched across to where the speaker stood. "These young people represent where we are now," he said. "Sometimes we lack self-respect and don't really care who we are. We have no goals or ideals to encourage us to do better. But we can bridge the gap."

The young couple then left the stage—but almost immediately they came on again, from the other side. This time they were well-dressed and clean. They held their heads up high, proud to be who they were. It was like magic! The crowd was electrified!

How did they get to the other side so quickly? How did they change their clothes and grooming so quickly?

The speaker had the audience in the palms of his hands. "We can be like this young couple," he said. "We can bridge the gap." As he said that, the bridge on the screen behind him suddenly became transformed. The center section appeared and the bridge was whole.

"All it takes is for us to cross the span from where we were—" and the unkempt couple stepped onto the stage—"to where we need to be." He gestured at the other, clean couple beside him.

The audience expelled its breath. The magician had been unveiled. He had used two sets of twins! But the magical moment was never lost. The audience always remembered the message the speaker was trying to convey.

Some time ago, Volkswagen ran an ad that was pure magic. It showed a photograph of their VW bus with a group of nuns getting in. The caption read "Mass Transit."

Reward and Punishment

A Masochist

Punishment

Reward

In every communication experience, the audience is going to ask one question: "What's in this for me?"

- The more people are rewarded for doing something, the more they'll keep on doing it.
- The more people are rewarded for learning, the more they'll keep on learning.
- The more people are rewarded for solving problems, the more eager they will be to solve problems.
- The more you want people to follow instructions, the more you reward them for following them.
- The more people are rewarded for change, the more they will change.
- The more results you get from communicating well, the more likely you will be to communicate.

A Critical Concept about People

People do things in proportion to the rewards they get. People also avoid things they get punished for and avoid them in the same proportional relationship. The following list contains the usual things people consider to be a punishment or a reward. The list was generated by advertisers to help them present products in terms of what the buyer wants. But it can be used to help anyone communicate better.

What Does the Audience Want?

to avoid effort	to save time
to make a lot of money	to be healthy
to be comfortable	to be popular
to enjoy pleasure	to be in control
to gratify curiosity	to be important
to satisfy an appetite	to be smart
to be a unique individual	to be praised
to have possessions	to avoid trouble
to feel blameless	to be in style
to be competent	to know why
to eliminate worry	to be happy
to be in a desired group	to be safe
to take advantage of opportunities	
to attract the opposite sex	
to emulate desired models	
to have a good reputation	

What Does the Audience Want to Avoid?

strenuous effort
losing time
losing money
discomfort
ill health
being neglected
pain
failing to be important
being dirty
losing possessions
being controlled
losing reputation
criticism
guilt
being stupid
trouble
being out of style
incompetence
boredom
failing to understand
danger
worry
being left out
unhappiness
repelling the opposite sex
being a mundane person
failing to emulate models
being unable to satisfy an appetite
failing to take advantage of opportunities

A person is always the center of the universe to himself or herself. One tends to look at everything from what can be gained from it—or what can be avoided. I do it, you do it, everyone does it.

This isn't bad—it's just the way we're built. Even acts of charity are performed because they make us feel good inside.

> *People are selfish; they are interested chiefly in themselves. They are not very concerned about whether the government should own the railroads; but they do want to know how to get ahead, how to draw more salary, how to keep healthy. If I were editor of this magazine, I would tell them how to take care of their teeth, how to take baths, how to handle employees, how to buy homes, how to remember, how to avoid grammatical error, and so on. People are always interested in human interest stories, so I would have some rich man tell how he made a million in real estate. I would get prominent bankers and presidents of various corporations to tell the stories of how they battled their ways up from the ranks to power and wealth.*
>
> John Siddwall, former
> editor of *American Magazine*

Toward Reward—Away from Punishment

People are attracted toward things they are rewarded for. They are repelled by things they are punished for. A good communicator will give rewards to help his audience receive his message. He will emphasize what they will get from it.

What is a reward, and what is punishment? Both are determined by the audience and their needs. When the communicator is able to take audience members closer to their needs, closer to satisfaction, he or she is giving a reward.

That is a secret to motivating people: clearly communicate to them how they will personally profit from what you offer.

How to Control the Situation

Comedians spend hours and hours practicing before they stand in front of an audience. They already know the jokes. So what are they trying to perfect? Two things, closely related: delivery and timing.

With timing you can have more control over how well your message is received. You can determine what the audience's reaction will be, whether relief or tension, fear or joy, anticipation or laughter, anger or excitement. Timing can heighten audience response, taking their normal response and multiplying it.

Most communication ignores the idea of timing. The communicator will take many ideas and try to cram them into one message. Much better would be to choose one idea and weave it in and out and through, like a single reed through a basket.

Time It Right

Timing is also related to overall audience awareness. People go through trends of thinking about a given subject. The time to talk about volcanoes is just after Mount St. Helens has erupted. The time to talk about presidential elections is during a campaign year. What if those are not topics you want to talk about? Tie your talk to the current trend. That's good timing.

Once the trend is over, drop it. Don't try to cling to it. That's bad timing.

This ad appeared in a newspaper:

> Whoever owns the '79 Mercury station wagon parked at SavMor Market, your lights are on.

The message was good, but the timing was bad.

The Responsive Line

Timing can be controlled by paying attention to the responsive line. The illustration below visually represents a responsive line. Assuming that a given communication is a line that runs from start to finish, the elements are units of time along that line.

First, grab the audience's attention. Then encourage and involve them. Then, and only then, present the core idea of your message. Expand on it. Give examples the audience can relate to. Then provide a summary so they'll retain what you've said.

Critical Factors

How does timing contribute to effective communication? Three critical factors must be remembered:

1 Placement: Where and how the communication is placed. Where and how the elements are placed within the message that's communicated.

2 Duration: How long it lasts. Each element can be critical. If it's too short, the audience won't quite keep up. If it's too long, they'll quit before the message is over.

3 Intensity: How strong it is. Make the message strong enough to hold interest and attention, but not so strong that it overwhelms.

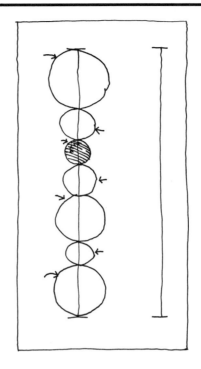

A communication piece can be visually planned by placing bubbles— which represent segments of time—along a time line.

When to start

How long

When to stop

Encouragement and Benefit

Redefine

Example-Specific

Central or Core Idea

Example-General

Memory Device-Retainer

Grab Attention

Digestion Rate

There is a limit to how much information a person can hold in one sitting, but we often try force feeding.

People have a limited capacity to digest information. (It's similar to digesting food). If a person tries to eat too much too fast, he will gag on the food, choke, and cough it out again. If he gets it all down, a lot of it will sour in his stomach, making him sick.

Information is the same. If we try to consume too much information at one time, it will either be rejected, not giving any benefit at all, or it will accumulate inside us until we get information indigestion. Anyone who has crammed for final exams knows this all too well.

Organizations usually equate volume with effectiveness. They seem to think that the more you can give the audience, the better.

That's pure hogwash, of course. Everyone has a digestion rate. If you exceed that, they'll throw it back up on you. How much will be retained? Nothing!

Gagging on Chemistry

I remember a chemistry class I took in college. Now, there's a place that really taxed my digestive system. Coming at me all at once was information about:

- a new environment
- new people (including a girl who looked interesting)
- a new language I was expected to learn
- a new subject
- in a new school

Result: I gagged on too much at one time and it came back up undigested. I flunked the course, of course.

The solution is to break up information into small pieces. How do you eat an elephant? One bite at a time. How do you hand out a huge amount of information? A bite at a time. Only then will the system be able to handle it.

Tools for Manipulating Your Audience

Learning Objectives Media	Factual Information	Visual Identification	Principles, Concepts, Rules	Procedures	Skilled Perceptual Motor Acts	Desirable Attitudes, Opinions, Motivations
Still Pictures	◑	●	◑	◑	○	○
Motion Pictures	◑	●	●	●	◑	◑
Television	◑	◑	●	◑	○	◑
3-D Objects	○	●	○	○	○	○
Audio Recordings	◑	○	○	◑	○	◑
Programmed Instruction	◑	◑	◑	●	○	◑
Demonstration	○	◑	○	●	◑	◑
Printed Textbooks	◑	○	◑	◑	○	◑
Oral Presentation	◑	○	◑	◑	○	◑

1

This generation has a choice of communications media unlike any before it. The communicator can make a presentation with support of everything from photographs to motion pictures to sound recordings to books. But all are not equally effective. The chart on this page shows which media are best for which functions.

● The dark circle indicates the most effective medium for the purpose noted.

◑ The medium circles are fair in their effectiveness.

○ The light circles are the least effective.

How to Warm Up a Relationship

If you're going to give a talk, look at the prior judgments the audience makes—before you even open your mouth:

"This guy's a little overweight. Fat people are dumber than thin people."

"I can tell this speaker is a scoundrel. I've never met a slick talker I could trust."

"That moustache makes him look like a sleazy car salesman. I remember the lemon I bought from a guy just like him."

"He looks like my favorite uncle."

"I'm glad she's talking about resumes. I need a good one."

"That Southern accent sounds phony."

The Audience Never Comes to You Cold

The audience will never come to you blank and empty. They, just like you, enter any communication situation with thousands of

A good speaker learns to de-ice an audience right away.

preconceived notions, with attitudes and opinions that will affect how they receive your message. You and your audience have a relationship going before you even begin to communicate.

There's not a great deal you can do about that prior relationship. But you can direct it into a new relationship that shows the audience they could well be wrong about you. Cultivate the soil before you plant the seed.

Look Before You Leap

Scouting out the audience in advance helps. Some misconceptions and misjudgments can be avoided. For instance, a movie called "Urban Cowboy" was not selling as predicted. Why? The problem, as one theater manager saw it, was the title. "Kids don't know what 'urban' means. I've asked dozens of them for their definition, and they think it means gay or homosexual. Who wants to see a movie called 'The Gay Cowboy'?"

What kind of person would race a car without first checking out the track and car?

What explorer wouldn't try to find a good map and talk to others who had been there before he leaves?

What politician doesn't test the water before he enters the race?

What communicator doesn't check out how the audience feels about both himself and the message before communicating?

I'm not sure of the answer to the first three questions but the answer to the last question is "most communicators." They just assume success. Do you?

The Key to Open the Mind

Present the same thing to several people and they'll all get something different out of it. Why? Because all come to it with different emotions.

Whether we like it or not, man is an emotional being. Some people like to think they're cold and mechanical and removed. "I'm just like a computer," a person told me once. "I can make decisions in a totally objective way. The facts are considered for what they are and emotions don't get in the way." Baloney!

Man Is an Emotional Being

Maybe some people think they can be completely logical—but they can't. Man is an emotional animal, and there is no way to escape that. Everything has an emotional tag. With the information, with the experience, comes the tag.

No Learning Occurs Without Involving Emotion

Thus, emotions can be excellent tools for the communicator. By using the emotions that are tagged to information and experience, the communicator can make sure that learning is occurring—and that it will be remembered.

The Past Is a Collection of Emotions

Think of the things you really remember from your past. Most of them are closely tied to an emotion. I remember touching a hot stove when I was little—and the feelings I had at the time: fear and anger. I don't remember the pain, but I do remember the emotion.

I remember being chased around a cherry tree by my mom. She had a big stick in her hand! Why do I remember that? The emotions.

I remember a math lesson I had in high school. I still remember what I learned there because the emotions were so strong that day. The teacher made us all laugh and feel so good that for years, in reminiscing, my friends and I would bring it up.

Emotional Communication

Emotions are living things, dynamic and ever-changing. People are never passive, even when they seem to be. Inside, they're active and alive. They aren't objective observers of communication. Invariably, they're emotionally involved (or emotionally uninvolved). When you approach them on the level of their emotions, you control the communication.

The End of the World

A friend of mine had a high school teacher who used emotion in teaching—and this friend still vividly remembers some of the lessons this teacher gave the class. One day the teacher decided to make the students feel something about atomic warfare. To prepare, he brought in a radio for a couple of weeks. While students worked on assignments, he played quiet music.

After the students were used to having the radio in the room, one of the teacher's friends rigged it so he could broadcast over that single unit—and he broadcast an announcement that the U.S. had just been attacked by nuclear missiles from the Soviet Union.

The teacher excitedly told the students they had better go home immediately. Just as they got up from their seats, the city fire alarm went off, as the teacher had prearranged.

You can imagine the reaction of the students! They ran out of the classroom and rushed down the halls toward the exits. At the last minute, the teacher stopped them. He explained what he had done and had them return to class.

To this day, they remember that lesson. My friend tells me he learned more in that one day than he did in entire courses in college. The reason is obvious: the teacher involved the students' emotions so much that the learning went in very deep.

Emotions—the Path to Our Soul

We are all vulnerable to different things. We are each open to different kinds of emotions. If a communicator can find out what emotions his audience will be particularly subject to, he has a real key to getting through to them.

Before trying to communicate with someone new, find out that person's attitudes, beliefs, tendencies, expectations, passions, and feelings. Then package the communication around those emotions.

It's not what happens to people that is important in any communication, but how they FEEL about what happens.

> *. . . the most important thing, as with any form of communication, is attitude. If you are trying to tell a person something, information is secondary to attitude. In order for human communication to occur, the transmitter must be pushing and the reception must be of value to the recipient, and you must make the people want the information you are giving them. If they do, communication will take place.*
>
> Bernard Bensen

The Most Common Mistake

When you work on a particular thing you feel strongly about, devote a lot of time to, and have part of your soul in, strange things happen. The project or idea gets inside. It creeps into the center of your chest and wraps itself around your heart. There it sets up housekeeping. It gets close, too close, and you can't see clearly anymore. You have lost all your ability to judge effectively.

There is no such thing as an objective human being (including you and me). Who you are colors everything you do.

My Way Is Everyone's Way

A common assumption people make is what is important to us is important to everyone else. We assume everyone sees things our way. But both assumptions are false. And both lead to faulty communication.

Myopia Made Easy

I like to paint, and more than once I've gotten so close to one of my paintings that I

*Has anyone seen my aardvark?
I can't find him anywhere!*

can't judge it. So my wife tells me what's wrong with it. Suddenly, what she's saying becomes obvious. Or I sometimes turn the picture upside-down, changing the perspective. That simple exercise distorts the drawing enough that I can lose some of my bias as the painter.

College texts are commonly written by professors, then required as texts for their courses. Students often complain: "I can't figure out what in the world this is saying." Why? Because the professor is so close to the subject and the book that he or she can't see that the communication is unclear.

For years, toothpaste companies thought people brushed their teeth to improve dental hygiene. They sunk millions upon millions of dollars into advertising campaigns based on that idea. They were simply too close to the problem. Studies later showed that people mainly used toothpaste to make their mouths feel better (though they would never say so)! Because the companies weren't really being objective, they told the public what they wanted to say—they communicated the wrong thing. Once one company made the shift to emphasizing how people's mouths would look and feel with their toothpaste, sales rocketed.

Seeing More Clearly

What can you do to avoid this kind of myopia? Some approaches help:

• Sit on your proposed communication for a while. Time has a way of revealing mistakes in thinking. Wait until you can see it with new eyes.

• Try to see it from another point of view. If you must, get outside input. Look at things the way your proposed audience would look at them.

• Try it out anyway. If it fails, then pick up the pieces and find out why. This is a very expensive approach. But burnt fingers teach even a dull mind not to touch the stove.

• Test it out with a portion of the intended audience. This seems obvious enough, but it is surprising how seldom it's done.

Newton's Law

A body in motion will tend to stay in motion.

Sir Isaac Newton developed the law of inertia: Once a body is in motion, it will tend to stay in motion.

This gives us an important principle. Every person on earth has habits—habitual ways of thinking, feeling, and acting. Once those habits are in motion, they'll stay in motion.

Most communicators have the nasty habit of confronting the audience directly, calling for them to change. Rather than fight against people's habits, however, it is much easier to use the power of habits to your advantage. When you link your new ideas to their old habits, your ideas become an extension of habit rather than a complete change in direction—and may eventually replace the habit altogether.

Try a Little Judo

This concept of inertia is used in judo. When your opponent comes at you, don't attack. Simply give way. Redirect the force of his own motion to take him to where you want him to go.

Don't fight other people's ideas and attitudes. Don't attack. Give way. Let the motion of their habits take them in the direction you want them to go.

People Are Habit Makers

- People are habitually chained to their past.

- People do things the way they've done them before.

- People believe things they've always believed.

- People like what's already familiar to them.

- People tend to read ads of things they've already purchased.

- People usually go to movies that are similar to ones they've liked in the past.

- People most readily understand things that are just like things they've seen and heard before.

Direct Change of Habits Is Always Resisted

Changing a habitual way of believing, doing, or feeling is a slow, hard process. The individual who changes overnight is very rare. The alcoholic who throws away the bottle never to drink again or the person who becomes an intellectual in a house that never has any books is the exception, not the rule. The majority of us are slow, very slow, to change a habit. We are all habit makers.

When anything interferes with that old comfortable way of doing things, people feel threatened. Especially when that thing is a direct confrontation. They will resist, fight, and scream their heads off to get it out of their path. Electric lights were thought to create disease and were resisted. Automobiles were a threat to man and beast and were resisted.

Nudge a Habit

With strength and brute force you can make people look like they're changing, but deep inside the fight goes on and habits remain the same. The solution is not to directly challenge or to stop anybody. Instead, go with the flow—go with their force and try to redirect it. It's easier to steer a car when sitting next to the driver than when in another car yelling and pointing and trying to force the car down a new road.

Kids love to play with Legos, those little plastic blocks that snap together. For some reason the Legos company doesn't like people calling the blocks Legos. As they point out in the brochure included in each package, they are properly "Lego Construction Blocks," and should be called that.

When you think about it, what they're asking is a little ridiculous. They're fighting people's habits. It would be much better

(and a far more efficient use of energy) if instead they were to use those habits for something constructive.

Every time my dad has a birthday, my mom gives him the same card. I'm not saying a new copy of the old card, I'm saying she actually gives him the old card again. And each time Dad reads it all the way through and says afterward, "How thoughtful! How nice!"

Of course, Dad knows it's the same card, and Mom knows he knows. But it's a nice habit they both enjoy; it's become a sentimental tradition for both of them.

There's no need to change that habit. But knowing about it helps. Can you think of some good ways a person could use that habit to help in communication?

Tie your communication to the audience's habits and they'll take what you have to say along with them. When what you're trying to communicate becomes part of their habit pattern, you've succeeded.

Intrinsic Crock

One man's garbage is another man's treasure. It depends on the perception of value.

Information has value in and of itself.
Dumb statement by famous person,
name withheld by request

Most speakers tell the audience what the speaker wants to talk about—and assume that is what the audience wants to hear.

Most people tell others things in language the teller understands, but fail to consider whether it is in language the listener can understand.

In other words, communicators concentrate more on the topic than on the audience!

The reason: there's a famous false belief floating around out there. It is that information has intrinsic value, that it is valuable just because it exists. Therefore, how it's communicated—and how it is received—doesn't matter.

The Value Is Within the Audience

Value doesn't exist intrinsically in anything. Value exists only as it's determined by the user. This applies to information as well as to anything else. The value of any information is determined by the audience, listeners, readers, viewers. If they decide that the information in question isn't helpful for them, then it holds no value.

It's Valuable Because "I Said So!"

Too often communicators pretend that they can set the value on the information they want to share:

"Pay close attention. This is an interesting idea."

"This is going to be a funny joke."

"This data is very important for you to receive."

"Everyone should learn Latin. It will greatly enhance one's education."

False, false, false. The data isn't important or the joke isn't funny just because someone said so. It's important or funny only when the receiver finds it so.

An example:

Everyone says driver's education cuts down on accidents. Take the statement at face value and it seems logical and believable. But Drs. Leon S. Robertson and Paul Zador of the Insurance Institute for Highway Safety did a study. They concluded that driver education usually doesn't cut down on accidents. In many states kids are allowed to begin driving at a younger age if they complete driver education. The lower age limit offsets the driver education courses. The result is that more accidents occur and more lives are lost.

Another:

The federal government requires that banks send out certain financial disclosures to their customers. The Minnesota Northwest National Bank was to send out 120,000 disclosures at a cost of $69,000. "It's stupid to send these out," they complained. "Our customers don't want to read this."

"It's the law," was the reply. "The information has intrinsic value."

So the bank complied.

But in the process Paul M. Eisen, one of the bank officials, did a little experiment. He put this paragraph in 100 of the disclosures:

"Any customer who receives a disclosure that includes this paragraph can get $10 simply by writing 'regulation' and the customer's name and address."

So far no one has collected.

People, Not Things, Determine It

The Bible, the faces on Mount Rushmore, the flag, and your neat idea have no value in and of themselves. Only people apply value (and in varying degrees) to things. Things only have value insofar as people assign it.

Value is a human concept. Value rests within the audience—and nowhere else.

Value here

Not here

Value is internal, not external. It is determined inside of each person.

Eliminating a Common Problem

A common communication problem: too much time and effort are spent on the subject—what you're going to say—and too little on how you want the audience to respond.

A good presentation is not enough. A good communicator's message causes the audience to act—to respond in a desired manner. Failure to elicit a response is failure to communicate.

The problem is one of putting the means over the ends. One of my kids was making whipped cream. But somewhere along the line, he got more concerned with the means than the end. He whipped and whipped and whipped that whipping cream until it was butter! He had forgotten that part of making whipping cream is knowing when to STOP whipping.

The means—the approach, the method, the way to communicate—are often given more attention than the desired ends. In fact, those ends—the desired results, the response, the impact, the why of the commu-

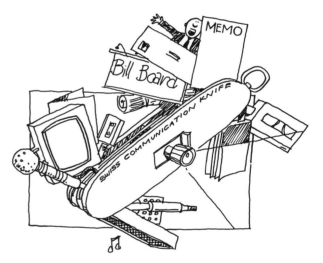

Putting the means before the end detracts from achieving desired results.

nication—are often not even considered!

You're Going to Hear What We Want to Tell You!

I once helped a government agency on a visitors' center they were planning. They had $2 million to spend; they wanted the latest equipment, the latest communication techniques—yet these are only the means to a communication end. They spent two years just planning the center.

A group of us did a rough check of the proposed audience. What would get results with them? What would have the greatest impact? The government's end goal was to "enhance visitor stays"—what would best do that?

We quickly discovered that visitors didn't want a visitors' center at all. They wanted a camp ground, boat docks, and picnic areas.

Unfortunately the agency, with an overriding preoccupation with means, went ahead as planned. And instead of whipping cream, they got butter.

Pretty Expensive Photography

A Hollywood director exhibited the same tendency to put means first. He was enamored with the film process; he wanted to do all that he could do—without spending any time learning if the audience would be interested when he was finished. He wanted to take pretty pictures more than entertain and involve the audience.

The result was $50 million down the drain—and an embarrassing bomb at the box office.

I have a close friend who used to work on a top-quality magazine, printed on slick paper and with a subscription rate of half a million.

But, unfortunately, the staff put means over ends. Instead of asking what the audience needed and wanted to read about, the staff told them what the staff thought they should know.

The result was that the staff accomplished what *they* set out to do. But they *didn't* communicate well with their audience. They didn't meet the audience's needs. They didn't accomplish the true goal of the magazine, which was to motivate, inform, and assist the readership. They were too busy taking care of the means.

First the Ends, Then the Means

In any communication, start by defining the ends. Learn what kind of response you want from the audience. What kind of impact do you want to have?

Once you know the desired end, you can construct your communication from that point and from that point only. All else—including specific subject matter—must remain secondary.

A Big Secret to a Big Impression

Pick up a photograph of a beautiful landscape with a girl off in one corner—and where does your eye immediately go? Right to the girl in the corner. **People identify with people.**

Personalities Promote Communication

People who have strong personalities enhance and dominate communication in their area of expertise. They become so well-known that their name almost becomes synonymous with their area of expertise. And their effectiveness and credibility increase at the same time. Look at this list:

- **Alfred Hitchcock** became the king of suspense/mystery movies.

- **Erma Bombeck's** name automatically evokes thought of homemaker-oriented humor.

- **Peter Drucker** dominates the field of business management.

A face can represent a thousand words.

- **Gloria Steinem** has become so well known for her efforts toward women's liberation that her name has become synonymous with her cause.

- **Adolph Hitler** and Nazism are so strongly linked that the mention of one automatically evokes thoughts of the other.

- **Dear Abby** has been so effective in her advice columns that you immediately think of her when someone says, "I was reading an advice column in the paper yesterday."

- **Elvis Presley** was the king of rock and roll—and after his death he still reigns.

- **Hugh Hefner's** name is inseparable from the hedonistic philosophy he advocates.

The Personalities Dominate

Some personalities become so effective in their field that others start to refer to the person rather than to the communication, to the creator rather than to the creation. That builds on the message those people wish to send.

When you view a painting by Picasso, Guernica for example, you don't say, "That's the painting about the bombing in the Spanish Civil War." Instead, you say, "That's a Picasso."

When Erma Bombeck comes out with a new book, her fans don't say, "Have you read such-and-such a title yet?" Instead, they ask each other, "Have you read Erma Bombeck's latest?"

Steven Spielberg's *Raiders of the Lost Ark* and other film efforts have been so successful that his name and personality have virtually come to stand for his work. "You've got to see such-and-such," people say. "It's by Steven Spielberg!" Those who have enjoyed his past movies know they'll enjoy the movies he makes in the future.

The more an audience identifies with the person or group communicating, the stronger the results will be.

A Vital Ingredient to Consider

Measuring dog food sales among cat owners doesn't give very accurate results.

One motion picture production company creates TV movies—but they screen and evaluate them in a theater. In a movie theater, people have a high level of expectation, they anticipate more involvement, they're affected by others in the audience, they're watching the show on a huge screen.

Compare that to the real context the movie will be seen in: small screen with a knob that makes it easy for the viewer to switch channels (or turn it off); distractions like kids running through, telephones ringing, or visitors at the door; a small screen and lots of commercial interruptions—all these things create a lower level of expectation and audience interest.

The company has had problems successfully capturing the TV movie market. And I think I know one reason why: they judge their productions in the wrong context.

The effectiveness of any communication is best evaluated in the context in which it will take place. And the more you know about the context, the better your judgment of the communication.

Outdated, Simplistic, and Naive

Leopold Kohr went on the lecture circuit for years giving his *Acres of Diamonds* talk. His point was that you don't have to wander the world to find wealth; you can find it in your own backyard. Nowadays many people think his ideas are outdated, simplistic, naive. But in their context, the ideas Kohr shared were valid. He gave the talk over fifty years ago when times were particularly tight economically. The talk must have been effective because over six million people came to hear it. When we judge Leo's presentation, it's only fair to consider *his* context, not ours.

2

Instructing the Employees

In South Africa, most of the men who work in the mines are illiterate. Management therefore uses simplified drawings to instruct or warn them. One such drawing, shown above, was an effort to enlist the miners' help in keeping mine tracks clear of rock and debris.

But the campaign failed miserably. The tracks became more and more cluttered. The reason: the miners were reading the message from right to left. Thus, they obligingly dumped their rocks on the tracks, just as they thought the sign was instructing them to do.

The managers of the mines had failed to consider the context in which they made their communication.

A Context of Circles

Things change when the context changes. Look at the circles in the illustration to see what I mean. Which of the two center circles appears larger? The one surrounded by the smaller circles does. But, in reality, both center circles are the same size. It's the context that makes the difference.

Gestalt

German psychologists have developed a great way of looking at things. Instead of trying to understand each individual part of something, they try to understand the whole.

This approach is called *gestalt* and means that nothing is ever an isolated entity. **Everything is an inseparable part of some larger context.** The same is true for communication.

3

Murphy's Laws

No matter how hard you try, there will be flaws in your communication. **No communication is ever completely successful.** Murphy's Laws prevail throughout life, and communication is not exempt.

Communication Failure

A survey has shown that 90 percent of television viewers misunderstand some part of what they see and hear. Somewhere the communication process breaks down. And it does so consistently.

In 1977 Jimmy Carter made a speech in Poland. His message never made it through translation. For example, his "desires for the future" became "lust for the future."

I once visited with an editor friend about his troubles with the communication process. He's a very careful man—but Murphy gets him, too. His worst mistake: he put the wrong author's name on a book.

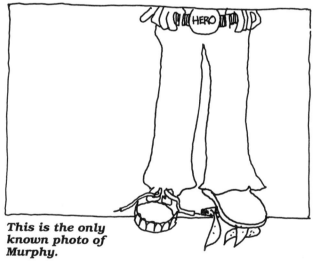

This is the only known photo of Murphy.

The Inevitable Breakdown

You can be as careful as you want, but inevitably something will go wrong. It's best just to do the most professional job possible, and then resign yourself to whatever problems arise. Communication is never 100 percent successful.

Maybe a few of Murphy's Laws will give you comfort:

• **Everything takes longer than you expect.**

• **Nothing is as simple as it seems.**

• **If anything can go wrong, it will.**

• **If there is a possibility of several things going wrong, the one that will cause the most damage will be the one to go wrong.**

• **Whenever you set out to do something, something else must be done first.**

• **Left to themselves, things tend to go from bad to worse.**

• **It is impossible to make anything fool-proof because fools are so ingenious.**

• **If a message can be understood in different ways, it will be understood in just that way which does the most harm.**

• **The probability of anything happening is in inverse ratio to its desirability.**

• **A shortcut is the longest distance between two points.**

• **Murphy was an optimist.**

from *Murphy's Law* by Arthur Bloch

A Way to Improve Any Communication

Employee Wheel

Management Wheel

Weak Management

Employees are not motivated or are not skilled

Effective Company

Compare a company to a bike and suddenly everyone understands more easily.

A manager of a small manufacturing plant was suffering through constant feuding between his plant workers and his office staff. Each group felt like its work was much more important to the successful operation of the company than the other group's work. The feud became so severe that production began to suffer seriously. Finally the manager called all the workers into one large meeting to try to resolve the problem.

"Our company is like a bike," he told them. "A bike has two wheels. If one of the wheels is smaller than the other, or if a wheel is missing altogether, the bike won't go right. But if both wheels are in balance with one another, it will move smoothly to its destination.

"In our company, we have two different shops. The office shop is one wheel on the bike, and the plant shop is the other wheel. If either wheel gets out of balance or broken the company can't move ahead."

Through the manager's explanation, the company workers were able to see how important *all* the workers were. The manager was able to communicate his ideas to his people because he used a metaphor.

A metaphor is the comparison of a familiar thing or idea with an unfamiliar. Metaphors are powerful communication tools—they can help solve a lot of communication problems.

Involving the Receiver

Metaphors automatically involve the audience—they make listeners a part of the presentation because they require that each individual visualize and interpret the metaphor for himself. Metaphors build a vital connection for the listener between the familiar and the unfamiliar, the known and the not known. They give your audience a vantage point from which to view new ideas.

A Historical Tree

One advertising council demonstrated the age of a tree by using a metaphor. They compared the rings from a cross-section of a tree to American history. By looking at this illustration a viewer could see how big the tree was when the Pilgrims dropped anchor in Plymouth Bay, how big it was when the Revolutionary War was won, when Lincoln was shot, and when the Wright brothers took off in their first airplane.

Once my kids came in complaining of squeaky bikes. "Go oil them," I said, and gave them some oil to do it with.

A while later I went out to check on how they were doing. They had oil all over the seats, the handlebars, and the fenders, not to mention their hands and faces. But none on the wheels or chains.

I figured it was time I teach my kids the facts of life as they related to oil. And the best way to do it was with a metaphor.

I had them bring me a board and some marbles. "Push the board across the cement," I told them. It made a lot of noise and moved stiffly. But I explained it would go across even smoother if they put some "oil" under it. "These marbles are like the oil you put on your bikes. Oil goes between things. So put the marbles between the board and the cement and see what happens."

It was smooth and easy. From the metaphor, they learned not only where to oil their bikes, but why.

Electrical Plumbing

Metaphors are all around us. All we need to do is reach out and grasp them. For example, an electrical system, which is poorly understood, is better understood when we compare it to a plumbing system:

Plumbing System	Electrical System
pipe diameter	wire gauge
faucet	outlet
water meter	electric meter
resistance	ohms
pressure	volts
flow	watts

You cannot have a ton of love, or a yard of hate, or a gallon of numinous awe; but love and hate and awe are just as real as a ton of flour or a yard of linen or a gallon of petrol, more real indeed, because they have immediate significance, they are not simply means to ends like making bread or pillow cases or haste.

Renee Hay

Wow 'Em!

A presentation with too much wow can overpower the message—and the audience may only remember the wow.

There's always a temptation to wow the audience with the presentation. We have a lot of technological pizzazz at our disposal nowadays—it's a real test of character *not* to overuse it.

If we're not careful, **the medium can overpower and destroy the message**. Then what happens? The audience walks away impressed with the presentation. And that's all!

An "I Dunno" with Pizzazz?

Not too long ago a huge exhibit opened up in the Northeast. It had laser lights and computer terminals and an exciting array of audio-visual support materials. The cost: $2 million. It attracted a lot of people, and they were all overwhelmed at what they had experienced.

A journalist decided to see how effective this state-of-the-art presentation was. He began to interview visitors as they left the exhibit. "What did you think of what you saw in there?"

"Wow, it was incredible! The neatest thing I've ever seen!"

"What was it about?" the journalist asked.

"Well—I dunno. But it sure was neat!"

Two million dollars to impress the people—and not even one to inform them, not even one to truly communicate. The exhibit, the journalist concluded, was nothing more than a "mindless parade of glitter."

The Medium Becomes the Message

Some communicators get so excited about the technology available to them that they forget their message. The medium becomes their message—but the message isn't what they wanted to send.

Some commercials on TV give a good example of this problem. They're so slick and impressive that the viewer never gets the message of the commercial. If you ask them what it was about they can't tell you. "I dunno," they'll say. "But it sure was neat!"

Some writers get so caught up in the beauty of their prose that they forget the story. The reader may enjoy the poetry, but totally miss the plot.

Some business presentations suffer the same affliction. They're so full of slide machines and sound effects and lighted wall graphs and other razzmatazz that the audience thoroughly misses the point.

Wowing people doesn't communicate, it only wows. It may grab attention. It may entertain, but it has a nasty habit of getting in the way of good communication. *Handle the lights, the buttons, and the pretty words with care.*

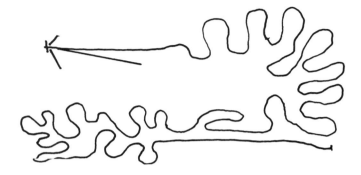

If you can't convince them, confuse them.

J. Scott Armstrong

Sometimes a presentation of an idea can have so much pizzazz that nothing gets though to the audience--except the pizzazz.

Opening Doors

Negative communication is harder to make effective. If possible, don't use it. It's not a good way to communicate with people. They won't get the full impact of what you're trying to tell them. The negative just doesn't get ideas across as well as the positive does. In fact, it is 50 percent slower in communicating.

Knock, Knock

Whenever people hear a negative, their brain automatically goes into overtime. First it has to process the idea of the negative. Then it has to switch to the positive.

Suppose a door reads "Do Not Enter." The person who sees the sign first considers the don't. "I shouldn't do something," he tells himself. Then comes the enter. "That's what I shouldn't do." The next computation: "If I shouldn't enter, then what do I do?" The answer: go a different way.

How much more effective the communication would be if the sign said, "Use Other Door." Still another way would be to emphasize

openness with the one door and closedness with the other. A glass door is more open and inviting, people are more apt to come in a partially open door, and clear graphics to enter help. If the desire is to discourage people from entering, the opposites of these are effective.

Positive communication makes the messages sent very clear!

I once had an office with a door in the wrong place. It would bring people right into my office from the hallway, instead of into the reception area. I tried just about everything, but to no avail. Leaving the door blank didn't work. Putting my name on it didn't work. It became a test in sign effectiveness. I would try a new sign, then see how many people came in.

Finally I tried two signs that worked better than the rest. The first one was "Women"; it stopped most people cold, except occasionally a surprised woman. Then I found the one that really did the job—no one came in. It was positive and offended no one. I even got lonely. The sign read, "Mechanical Room."

Come In

Why all this talk about doors? What do doors have to do with communication?

Isn't opening door the real essence of all communication effort? Once a person's door opens, both in real and in metaphorical terms, your work is half over.

Emphasize the positive, de-emphasize the negative. The problem with a negative approach is that negative emotions are easy to create. And once created, they become affixed to you and your message. You may open the door with something negative, but often it will slam shut on your fingers.

The positive is always easier to internalize than the negative. It's a stronger force. It creates positive emotions by communicating more directly and more effectively. It gets the point across quicker and more emphatically. The door is easier to open and stays open longer. Going in and out of an open and inviting door is always easier.

A Technique to Refine Your Presentation

Why and how are words so important that they cannot be used too often.
Napoleon Bonaparte

Our language has certain key words that will open up information—and the ways to communicate that information. Those words all come in the form of questions. They help us understand what we need to do to make our communication work.

The Question Words

What? What is the message to be communicated?

Where? Where will the communication take place?

When? At what time (of the day, of the year, in what era and social climate) will it occur?

Why? What is the purpose of the communication? What do I want the audience to do as a result of this communication?

Who? Who will be receiving the communication? Who is the audience?

How? How will the message be communicated?

> *I had six honest serving men—they taught me all I knew. Their names were where and what and when and why and how and who.*
>
> Rudyard Kipling

Which? Which of all the ideas will be presented? What is their priority?

Well? Well, how did I do? (To be asked after the communication has been completed.)

Every communication can be strengthened and refined by asking these questions in advance. If the communicator will take the pains to find intelligent and complete answers to each question, the communication will be more successful.

An Ingredient That's Often Overlooked

The speaker stands up, hesitant and fearful. He frowns down at the audience. They frown back up at him, hesitant and fearful. He gives his speech in a halting voice, finally sits down.

The next speaker gets up. He's buoyant, enthusiastic. He smiles broadly and begins to speak excitedly. The audience undergoes an amazing transformation. They sit more comfortably in their seats. They smile at the speaker; they lean forward in their chairs, hanging on his every word.

Your audience will tend to reflect the level of your interest, enthusiasm, and motivation right back to you. If you're interested and excited about your subject, the audience will share in that interest and excitement. If you're bored or unmoved the audience will reflect that boredom and lack of emotion back to you

Mirror Image

An audience is like a mirror. When you look in it, you see what you send. If you send love, you get love back. If you send enjoyment, you get enjoyment back. If you send doubt, you get doubt back. If you send confusion, you get confusion back.

If you don't believe in your subject, or if you're not really interested in it, don't bother trying to communicate it. You'll just be

wasting your time. Your audience won't believe it or be interested in it either. A mirror never lies.

Little Hulks

My kids were once watching The Incredible Hulk on TV. When the hero was provoked, he'd turn into the monstrous green Hulk, ripping off his shirt in the process. Right after the show my kids started playing Hulk—complete to the point of ripping off their shirts, buttons flying everywhere.

What my kids were doing was nothing more than reflecting back what they saw. They were the perfect audience. They became what they saw.

Reflecting Back

Everyone is the reflective audience. Adults are more restrained, of course, but they invariably send back what they receive. Smile at people. What do they do? Smile back, virtually every time.

What do you want from your audience? Make up your mind—then give them what you want them to give you. You'll get back what you send, many-fold.

Nothing is a greater impediment to being on good terms with others than being ill at ease with yourself.

Honore de Balzac

WARNING　　　WARNING

Try never to communicate something you're not interested in or don't believe in; your audience won't be interested and won't believe it either.

Power of the Situation

A situation can greatly influence how people act.

Suppose you were invited to a free seminar at your friend's house. The speaker: your friend. She gives you some information on how to invest successfully in real estate. The ideas seem good, but you're not so impressed that you write home about it.

Suppose, on the other hand, that you were invited to a seminar at a classy hotel. The cost for four hours of instruction: $200. The speaker: a world-famous real estate investor. You take notes as fast as you can write, hanging on every word. Then you go out and try to apply what was taught.

Guess what—the information at both seminars was exactly the same. The only difference was the situation.

A group of people is watching a comic on the stage. He tells a joke—dead silence. The next night he tells the same joke to a new group and they crack up laughing. Same comic, same stage, same joke. What was the difference? The situation. Laughter is contagious, and once a few people got it rolling it was hard to stop.

A teacher stands before her high school English class. She is an excellent teacher. But the situation is against her. The kids feel peer pressure to act up, to disparage the subject. No matter what the teacher does, she loses.

The Situation Dictates the Response

People invariably respond to a situation in a way that matches their own definition of that situation. They act in a drugstore the way one is supposed to act in a drugstore. They act at a baseball game in a very different way—but it is the way one is supposed to act at a baseball game.

Try to control the situation or it could control you.

How to Cue Up an Emotional Response

A cue is something that causes a person to recall an experience from his memory. We all have thousands of things stored in our memory banks; the cue triggers our brain to remember them at a particular point. The cue raises the memory from the subconscious into the conscious mind—and there it can have a much more profound effect on us.

- I grew up on a farm. The smell of new-mown hay makes me relive days when I was younger.

- A particular sentence overheard recalls the words often said by a friend—long dead.

- A foggy day makes one person remember a forgotten love.

- Seeing a cleaning product in the store causes you to remember the time you spent two days on your hands and knees scouring a stubbornly dirty floor.

- Driving at night in the rain, the windshield wipers silently flapping, brings back a melancholy evening of long ago.

- A cliche brings to mind a history teacher I had in high school—who must have used that cliche at least once a day.

- A kitty causes someone to recall memories of childhood.

- A certain smell in conjunction with hunger pains causes you to salivate.

All Action on Cue

Hypnotists know the power of the cue. While their subject is still in the hypnotic state, the hypnotist tells him that he'll perform a certain action—sing, maybe, when the hypnotist snaps his fingers. The subject wakes up. He forgets all about the command the hypnotist gave him. But then the hypnotist snaps his fingers. The cue has been given, and the subject, whether he wants to or not, has the memory of the command move from his subconscious to his conscious. He starts to sing.

The cue is a powerful communication tool. People's experiences are closely tied to their emotions, and emotions are usually what cause us to act. How can the communicator stir his audience's emotions? By pushing the right cue button.

Cue Up an Emotion

The communicator can have a lot of goals. He or she wants the audience to buy something, or think something, or do something, or change their ways. The quickest way to get any of that to happen is to go straight for their emotions. And the most direct route to the emotions is the right cue.

Suppose you want to persuade a mother to buy a toy for her child. The trick may not be to convince the mother that the child would like or enjoy the toy. Instead, it's to get the mother to remember how she felt when she got a new toy as a child. Push the cue button, get her to re-experience that memory. Suddenly she remembers the joy and excitement of getting a new toy, and she wants her child to have the same feelings. Success!

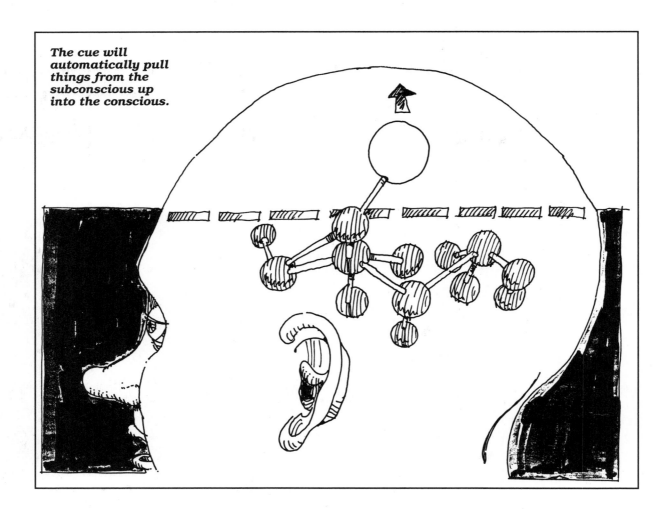

The cue will automatically pull things from the subconscious up into the conscious.

Get a Grabber

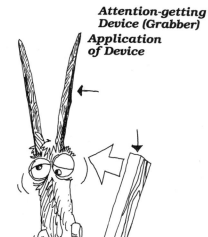

The best way to get someone's attention is to grab it with something.

Grabber (Grab-ber) n. An attention-getting device used at the beginning of any communication to get others to listen to a message.

A Little Attention Grabber

The way to get someone's attention is to use a grabber. An old farmer in my area is well known for his ability at training jackasses. In fact, he became so famous for his way with the animals that he was visited by state agricultural officials. "Jackasses are famous for being very cantankerous. How in the world do you train them so quickly?" they asked.

"Well," the old farmer drawled, "it's really not so hard. It takes a little expertise, of course. But it's more a matter of emphasis than anything else. In fact, I'll bet just about anybody could do it. Training jackasses isn't much different from working with people."

The officials looked at him stupidly. "What are you trying to tell us?"

"Well," the old farmer drawled, "I guess I'll just have to show you." He picked up a 2" x 4" board off the ground and whacked the nearest jackass over the head, hard.

"Hey, wait a minute," the head official said. "I thought you were really good with animals."

"I am," the farmer replied. "But first you have to get their attention!"

Before you can get through to someone else, you first have to get their attention. This principle is well understood in our society, even though we don't recognize it often enough. Look at some of our sayings and you'll see what I mean:

You can't save souls in an empty church.

People won't walk inside if the front door is locked.

Everybody wants to follow the fire truck.

Everybody hears his own name.

Any jackass can be made to take notice.

Get Attention First

Once you've got someone's attention, you can give them your message. But until you have their attention, you won't be able to communicate a thing.

Everything else in communication is secondary to this principle. You might have the best ideas in the world. You might have the most exciting presentation that's ever been prepared. But until you have the attention of your audience, nothing else matters. You might as well have manure in your briefcase as that sparkling slide show.

Methods That Grab

So you want to grow up and be a grabber! How do you do it? Here are a few different approaches that can work for you:

Be Complex
Start your presentation with a lot of richness, with depth. Give the audience a lot to see or think about. Once you're into your presentation, be simple. But you can be complex to grab them.

I've seen this idea applied in many different ways. I was once at an art show that featured abstract paintings. It was obvious which pieces of art grabbed the viewer the most: the most detailed ones. The more complex the art, the more time the people gave to it.

Think about the movies you like to see over and over again. It's a pretty safe bet that you return to the richer ones. You find that complexity intrigues and interests you.

Unless you're making a movie, you can't sustain ninety minutes of complexity in your communication. But you certainly can begin with it.

Be Visual
Dominate the audience's sense of sight. I've seen over and over how effective simple visual touches can be. The person who speaks with a large chalkboard or sheet of paper handy, recording key points on the board as he goes, is the one who invariably ends up dominating the meeting.

We're living in the TV Age—two generations now have been reared with television. That kind of exposure has created a tremendous demand for the visual aspect of communication. Many audiences are at a loss if they don't receive visual input along with the verbal.

If you include visual elements in your presentation, you'll be two steps ahead of those who don't. But if your competition "out-visuals" you, watch out!

Have Movement
Early survival of both man and animal depended on when to move and when to stand still. Mankind still has those survival skills. And they apply to effective communication.

The time to move around is at the beginning of your presentation. Use plenty of gestures and body language. Pace. Use good physical expression. You can settle down later, if appropriate. But grab at the beginning with excited movement.

I can still remember a speech I heard years ago. I remember the name of the speaker, what was said, and how he said it. His topic wasn't that unusual, but his presentation was. He used movement—in the form of dancing girls. He sent up balloons. He used a lot of gestures.

The first thing you see in any setting is what moves. Couple your message with movement to make it memorable.

Be Obscure

If you're obscure in an intriguing way, the audience will be right with you as they try to figure out what you're up to. Everyone loves a guessing game. Look at the popularity of TV game shows—most are different forms of guessing games. Charades is a favorite at parties. Why? Because people love to play guessing games.

Involve your audience in a genuine guessing game, grabbing them in to your message.

Threaten Punishment

Think back to when you were a kid. You're supposed to be mowing the lawn, but it's so hot outside that you just can't get too enthused. So you lie down under a tree and start to daydream.

Then your dad comes out with a grabber and captures your attention real quick: you see him standing in front of you twitching a willow.

The same idea can be applied as a grabber in other settings. Most threats will be for punishment that you couldn't apply. Get the audience to fear financial collapse, failure, loss of opportunity.

The dominant emotion I feel from people (I'm sorry to say) is fear. That's unfortunate—but you can turn fear to your advantage, using it as a grabber in your communication. And maybe by the time you've finished giving your message, the people won't be so afraid anymore.

Be Reflective

People are most interested in what they need and in what they fear. Reflect those feelings back to them and you've got a good grabber.

We spend a lot of time seeing reflections of ourselves in all we do. We hear a lecture and think the communicator is talking just to us—or that the message is totally off the beam. We read a book and think it's the greatest thing ever written because it speaks just to us. Or we put it down, disgusted that we wasted our money on such a piece of junk.

The difference is how well the message or the book reflects our needs and feelings. When something gives order and form to our feelings, we listen. Reflect the audience's feelings, needs, fears, and they will be with you.

Promise a Reward

Most of us spend our lives reaching for a golden ring. When someone promises to help us, we give him our complete attention. I remember two talks I heard in church. Talk 1 discussed who God is and what the afterlife will be like. The audience was only mildly attentive.

Then the second speaker began. He talked about money and human relations—and how religion could help. The audience sat enraptured, giving their complete attention.

Here's a simple concept to keep in mind: **People are interested in what's on their minds.** If they talk and think about something a lot, you can be sure they're interested. Are people interested in the afterlife? Yes, but not nearly so much as they are in money and human relations in this life! The immediacy of today always dominates the possibility of tomorrow. Promise people a reward. Help them see that you'll deal with what concerns them most, and you'll grab their attention.

Use Contrast

Contrast your presentation with your environment, or use contrast in the presentation itself, and certain items will stand out. Identify the context of the situation you'll be in, then break out of that mold to grab the audience.

Contrast is created by doing something out of context. Above, the black circle stands out because it is out of context. Below, the jagged line is the one that catches your attention.

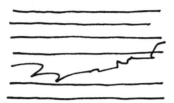

Contrast is relative to context. A man in a top hat and tails might not be too noticeable at a formal Presidential ball—but put him in a nudist camp! Then he's the first thing you see. Employ contrast.

Be Unique
Give the audience stuff that's strange, one of a kind, never seen before. Make them feel that you're going to let them in on some secrets that have never been revealed before. P.T. Barnum used this approach over and over with his bearded lady and midgets.

Ripley's Believe It or Not sold millions upon millions of copies—all because it promised something unique.

The ten o'clock news uses the idea, too. Just look at the kinds of grabbers they'll throw at you: "Astronauts go to Mars. Three million people have starved to death in Bangladesh. Airplane crash kills 500. Details at ten."

Grabbing attention is essential. If you don't grab their attention, something else will. Either you have their attention or you don't.

Ways to Maintain Interest

Communication must maintain the interest of the audience. If a message fails to hold their interest, it will not hold their attention—and learning or change will not occur.

What Affects Interest?

• **Generation, age, era.** History usually bores the young because they can't relate to it. If you must talk about something that is removed by time, either bring the subject into today, or take the audience into yesterday.

• **Current events.** In the '60s, free love was a favorite theme. But in the '90s, we are worried about safe sex and the threat of AIDS. In the McCarthy era, everyone was on the lookout for communist sympathizers—but now we talk about glasnost and perestroika. Such events dramatically shape our attitudes and expectations.

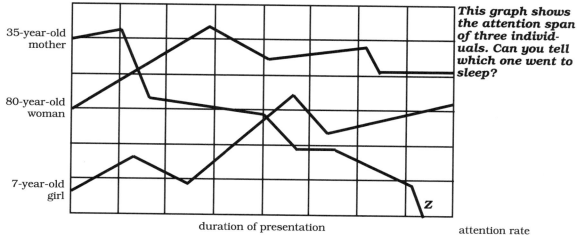

This graph shows the attention span of three individuals. Can you tell which one went to sleep?

35-year-old mother

80-year-old woman

7-year-old girl

duration of presentation

attention rate

• **Trends, fads, and fashions.** Things are no longer groovy—they are rad or rippin'. Sixties nostalgia is a popular theme for music, movies, parties, and advertisements, but in ten years an ad reminiscent of the sixties may miss the mainstream population altogether.

• **Proximity.** How close to the audience's lives has your topic reached? The closer the topic or concern, the more interested they will be. For example, people in Nebraska are probably not too concerned about how to handle a volcanic disaster. Likewise, people on the west coast don't worry about twisters and hurricanes.

When you tailor a message to the interests of your audience, they will reward you with their attention.

How Do You Maintain Interest?

1 Find the audience's interests. What do they spend their time doing? What are their greatest concerns in life? What do they worry about the most? What are they happiest about? Then talk about it. The most interesting subject in all the world is ourselves.

2 Keep current. Interest and attention are dynamic and ever-changing. An audience is not interested in the same things forever. This week's interests may be passé next week. The mother who talks to her daughter the same way now as she did ten years ago is not communicating. A broken record could do as well.

3 Use emotion. The way to meet people's interests is to approach them through their emotions—what they feel. The heart and mind are inseparable. The heart is the best route to the mind.

4 Find the common interest. Keep in mind that interest is a relative thing and that it differs from person to person. Any audience will almost certainly be made up of people of many different backgrounds and many different interests. Ask yourself what the common threads are that run through the entire audience. Then weave those same threads through the communication.

5 Capitalize and awaken. Interest comes in varying levels. Some people will be consciously interested in something that others are interested in only subconsciously. A presentation should be designed so as to capitalize on the interest of those who know they're interested—and to awaken the interest of those who are less obviously involved.

6 Identify a target audience. The broader the appeal you make, the less intensity of interest you can hold. You can interest both an 8-year-old boy and an 88-year-old woman at the same time. But it is easier to hold the interest of each one individually. Identify a specific audience and aim your message directly at them. By concentrating on a specific audience with common interests you can more easily hold the attention of everyone.

7 Be flexible. Experiment. Play. Interest can be destroyed by the habit of repeating only past successes. What *has* worked may not be what *will* work in the future.

E.B. White, when commenting on effective writing style and approaches, said, "The only crime is to bore the reader." The only crime in any communication is the same—boredom.

This Limits All Communication

A jungle native won't be able to understand snow—unless he experiences it—because there is nothing like it in his experience.

Every person on earth has a severe limitation that dominates and overrides every other capability. The limitation: **People can only interpret information in terms of what they know and have experienced.**

What's Snow to a Jungle Native?

Think of how difficult it would be to describe snow to someone who had never seen or experienced it. You go into the jungles of equatorial Brazil and talk to one of the natives. You've mastered the language—but the man has never seen snow. He doesn't have a refrigerator with frost in it; he hasn't seen pictures in books or magazines; he's never traveled anywhere. Even if the native's language has words for cold, you're going to have a tough time communicating the idea of snow to him. He simply has nothing in his experience that will help him understand.

Experience and knowledge add meaning. If an audience fails to relate their experience to your ideas, they won't be able to understand what you're saying. The meaning of their experiences adds to your message.

Attempting the Impossible

A lot of would-be communicators waste a lot of time trying to do the impossible. They ignore the experience/knowledge limitation of their audience and bravely plunge in. But it's about as effective as speaking in Chinese to a Laplander or telling a newborn baby about higher mathematics. Without experience and knowledge, the audience simply doesn't have the necessary background to pull meaning out of the communicator's message.

Base what you have to say on what the audience already knows.

How to Increase Your Impact

The more you identify with your audience, the more impact you will have on them. You will be able to influence them more in their problems, motives, and needs. You will be able to show them that you know what they're all about.

Going to the Dogs

Be sure you try to relate to the real audience, though. Who eats dog food? Not people—dogs! So who's the real audience for dog food? It's not dogs. It's people. Because only people buy dog food.

One marketer of dog food developed a brand that really tasted good to dogs. It did an excellent job of reproducing (as far as anyone could tell) the taste and smells of a dog's more natural food. The marketer expected the sales of his dog food to shoot right off the chart. But it never even got off the ground. Why? Because it smelled dead. People don't like to think their dogs are eating dead stuff (even though dogs often do).

What was the problem? He was going after the wrong audience. To succeed, dog food needs to appeal to people, not dogs. It could taste so bad that the dog would gag on it, but if it appealed to the dog's master, that's what the dog would get.

Know the Audience

Ask yourself questions like:

Am I talking Plato, Dewey, and Spinoza when my audience wants Peanuts, Dear Abby, or football? or vice versa?

Am I using big words when only small ones will be understood?

Am I talking about stocks and bonds to a welfare recipient? Or saving acccounts to a high roller?

The Strongest Form of Communication

What if you could talk one-to-one with Clyde Scheckle in all these media? Boy, you'd have him HOOKED!

The more each member of your audience feels you are talking to him alone, the more effective your communication will be. Give each member of the audience the feeling that you're sitting down with him for a private, one-to-one talk and he'll be completely responsive and totally interested.

Here's Talking to You

Suppose you went into a bookstore and there was only one book on the shelf. The cover read, "This book's for you"—and then it said your name. Would you buy the book and read it? You bet you would!

Suppose you went to a seminar and the speaker said, "Everyone who is not named _____ (your name), please leave." Do you think you would stay to hear what he had to say?

Of course, both of those situations are impossible. But the speaker or writer can speak personally with the audience. Get to know their fears and concerns, their needs and hopes, and then talk about them. Be personal. Talk directly to each one. Repeat things they've said. Show them solutions to their problems. Before you know it, each person in the audience will feel you're talking to him or her alone.

Have you ever been to a movie where you were so involved that you forgot it was a movie? You felt as if you were actually a part of the action!

Have you ever heard a speech in which the speaker got you so involved that you felt that just you and he were in the room? Or that the message was just for you?

It's all a matter of getting the audience to feel one to one with the communicator. There's a children's book available that's totally personalized. It's an excellent concept. Each custom-made book includes the name of the child who's receiving the book, as well as names of his friends and pets, as characters in the book. Talk about getting involved with the communication! Kids love and cherish those books. It is truly their book. It talks about them, to them.

101

Generalization vs. Specialization

The more generalized your information and approach, the less power you'll have. The more you can talk to one person—using his name, basing your communication on his experiences, and solving his problems—the better.

The strongest communication is one-to-one; all else is a compromise. To generalize is weaker, but allows you to talk to more people. To specialize is stronger, but restricts the number of people who are interested in the message.

How to Increase the Value of Your Message

A lot of failure in communication comes when the communicator tries to do it all. He tries to do everything by himself, denying the audience the chance to contribute. In doing so he denies himself the chance to succeed.

Communication is a two-way process. If it's one-sided, it really isn't communication at all. The more an audience participates in the communication, the more they'll get out of it. The effective communicator will plan ways that will allow the audience to be as involved as possible in the communication process.

A good pantomime artist uses this principle, going through motions that indicate things to the audience. But the audience must fill in the gaps themselves. The mime gets the audience to see things that aren't really there, to feel things that are only suggested.

Fill in the Blanks

If the communicator allows his audience to fill in the blanks, refusing to do all their work for them, he'll find that the message gets across much more effectively. Blanks for the audience to fill in get the audience more involved and more excited about the message presented.

Fill in these blanks:
Roses are red, violets are _____.
A bird in the hand is worth _____.
I pledge allegiance to the _____.
Raindrops keep falling on my _____.
Dum, dum, dee, dum, dum— _____.

The British Broadcasting Co. once conducted a survey on the audience perception of British television. One of the respondents, a young boy, said he preferred radio. "The pictures are better," he explained.

Why? Because radio allowed him to fill in the blanks. It allowed him to participate to a greater degree.

Let Them Participate

I once helped design a Strategic Air Command exhibit. We included a display that called for more participation than other displays. It allowed people to climb into a cockpit where they could actually push buttons and imagine themselves flying the plane. We weren't too surprised to learn that over the years that display needed more maintenance than others. People were eager to do more than look and listen.

The same idea applies to all communication. Let the audience do more than look and listen. Let them participate. They'll become more interested in the message, and it will make a more lasting impression on them as well.

Participation produces the ultimate in communication: you know you've succeeded when the audience comes back to you and thanks you for bringing out certain ideas. And the ideas weren't even in your communication!

"That was neat the way you pointed out the intelligence of the housewife," one says.

"I appreciated your saying that skills once attained are never lost," says another.

Yet you said nothing of the kind. So where did the audience get those ideas? From themselves! They were participating with you to the extent that they didn't draw the line between your words and their thoughts.

When you hear those kinds of comments, you'll know your communication has really worked.

If you teach a man everything, he will never learn.

George Bernard Shaw

I hear and I forget. I see and I remember. I do and I understand.

Old Chinese saying

. . . words that make pictures in the mind and pictures that make words in the mind.

Draper Daniels

Never Do This!

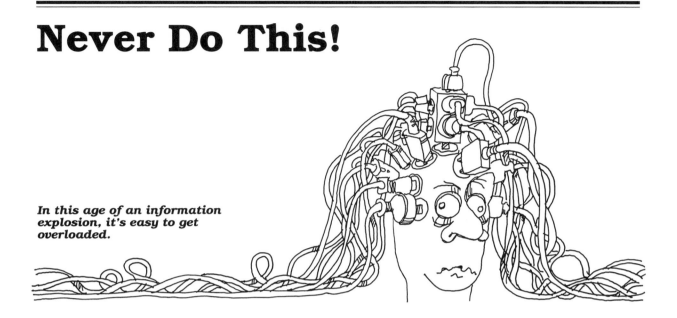

In this age of an information explosion, it's easy to get overloaded.

During the past year alone:

- over 40,000 books were published
- over 300,000,000 pieces of mail were handled by the postal department
- over 100,000 technical reports were printed
- over 25,000 hours of television programming were produced
- nearly 2,000 messages were sent to each adult every day

We're suffering from a classic case of overload. Add to the list above the amount of new stuff that came out the year before. Then add the stuff that will come out this year.

Every eight years the amount of information that is accumulated doubles. Not even a super computer could keep up with that.

The more messages are sent, the less true communication there will be. There is a limit to the amount of information we can take in at one time.

Some people try to communicate all they know—at one sitting. It's impossible (unless they don't know much!). When they try to tell too much, their listeners start to suffer from communication overload. Their minds are getting more input than they can assimilate. Result: more and more is said and less and less is understood.

I work on the assumption that in the crowded mass communication field today you have to get in and get out with your message quickly and as simply as possible. You must communicate the maximum with a single glance.

Saul Bass

Lightening the Load

Here are some steps to avoid contributing to the overload problem:

- **Be Bold.** Make your message stronger, make it stand out more boldly than the others.

- **Be Concise.** Get right to the point. Be more concise than anyone else.

- **Be Aware.** Know your audience. Make your message fit them better. Give them more of what they want.

- **Be Clear.** Make your message easy to understand. Eliminate unnecessary words, phrases, and ideas.

- **Be Simple.** Make it simpler. Most people can assimilate only seven different pieces of information at a time.

In this age of overload, consumers and listeners are becoming more selective than ever about information. They want something easy to understand and relevant, or they will ignore it.

We live in an electronic age in which
information travels at the speed of light.
Marshall McLuhan

Pay Close Attention to This Detail

Information is transported by communication just as cargo is transported by trucks.

Too many communicators are confusing the message to be communicated with the communication process itself. For example, a friend of mine lived in South America for a year. Her parents sent her a very nice package for Christmas—it contained presents, food, candy, letters, and books. But they sent it in November by slow boat! She received the Christmas package in April. The message was good, but the medium for communicating it could have been improved.

Trucking Your Ideas

The relationship between communication and information (the message) can be better understood by making a comparison with a truck. The communication is the truck itself, and the message is the cargo inside. The message is what you're sending from yourself to others, and the communication is the way you send it. The communication is the carrier.

How you send a message is just as important as what message you send. Good, timely, interesting messages can be made useless when sent the wrong way. Presidential press conferences, for example, are never aired at 3:00 a.m. for a very good reason—few people would see them. They are usually shown during or after the dinner hour, when the most voters will be at home watching TV.

Transport Questions

Carriers come in basically two forms or media. The first is software, such as metaphors, analogies, stories, and live presentation. The second is hardware: books, video discs, pictures, and the like.

In choosing the vehicle to carry your message, here are some basic questions to ask:

- Is the vehicle reliable? Will it get you to your destination without breaking down? For example, don't choose a story that is so long people forget the topic before you finish.

- What are the vehicle's capabilities? You would pick a train or truck for land, a boat

107

for sea, and a plane for air transport. In communications, movies and visuals are good for some situations, stories and activities for others.

• What size vehicle is needed? You don't need a semi-trailer to transport a crate of oranges. When communicating, don't use a movie when one photograph will do.

• What experience do the drivers have? You wouldn't select a trucking company whose drivers were inexperienced or accident prone. If you are going to rely on other people, materials, or machines to deliver your message, be sure you know their abilities.

• What route is best? Is your vehicle able to cover the route you've chosen? Are your directions clear?

• How is the traffic? When you deliver your message, will you encounter background noise? It is hard to sell a product to a buyer who is continually being interrupted.

• What is the proper speed? Does your truck have enough speed and power to arrive on time? Does your communicating medium meet the time requirements? Will your audience wait for the message to reach them? Or does your communicating vehicle move so fast that it goes right by without your audience being able to get the message?

• Can you be hijacked? Will someone or something else take your vehicle down the wrong route? Can what you are communicating be turned against you?

Different kinds of communication require different media or vehicles. For instance, you could transport the same information cargo in a radio drama, a story book, a newsletter, or a TV show. The information would be basically the same, but the vehicle and the audience response would be drastically different in each case.

A Subtle Way to Enhance Your Message

Symbols are the carriers of ideas between people.

It is through symbols, and only through symbols, that we are able to communicate. This book, for example, is full of symbols. In fact, that's all it contains. Each letter symbolizes a sound; each word symbolizes a meaning. Each illustration symbolizes a concept.

Effective communication comes through using symbols in a way that's meaningful to both sender and receiver.

Our dollar bill is a symbol of economic value. Dollar bills don't have any value in themselves, but the symbol is so powerful that we all spend a good part of our lives trying to acquire an extensive collection of them.

Shaking the head symbolizes the negative.

The swastika and the cross are two such symbols, both very similar in design but very different in meaning.

> Symbol: Something that stands for or suggests something else.

Hand symbols are used to communicate:

victory sign   OK   number one
(but don't try
this one in Italy!)

This illustration is effective because the viewer is able to make a mental transfer of symbols that have become meaningful to him.

A nod on the head symbolizes an affirmative response.

Crossed arms and legs in a conversation may symbolize that the listener disagrees with the person talking.

A warm handshake symbolizes friendliness.

Smells can communicate in symbols. Lilacs, for instance, symbolize the newness and freshness of spring.

Wide-open eyes have come to symbolize astonishment—or horror.

The song "The Halls of Montezuma" has come to symbolize military service and war.

Symbols are Mind Tools

It's important to remember that the meaning isn't in the symbol itself, but in the person who sees the symbol. The meaning you get from this book isn't on the page but is in your head.

Consider these things when using symbols:

• what the symbol means to your audience.

• what response the symbol will evoke from the audience.

• what context that meaning and response require. (Our dollar bill will be meaningless in Lapland. To them it's just a piece of paper.)

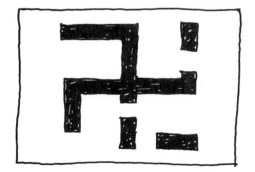

These drawings show only parts of famous symbols. Yet the symbols have become so well known that even a portion does the work of the whole.

Stopping the Memory Curve

NOW, WHERE DID I LEAVE MY HAT?

People easily forget things they learn. And quickly. In fact, sometimes people forget in less time than it took them to learn! Within a single day the average person forgets a full two-thirds of what he's learned. Most of the rest is gone within a month. This problem has been plotted as a memory curve: the more time passes, the lower the line drops down into the forgotten section of the curve.

A message that isn't remembered is useless. It's not valid in the least unless the audience remembers it. To stay in the remembered part of the graph try these ideas:

• **Repetition.** The more you want people to remember what you have to say, the more times you tell them. William Randolph Hearst described the approach as follows: "First you tells folks what you're gonna tell 'em; then you tells 'em; then you tells 'em what you told 'em."

When a doctor wants to immunize some-one against a particular disease, he gives a shot—then gives booster shots periodically to make sure the vaccine took effect. The communicator must follow the same process. Give the information initially—then repeat it over and over to make sure the listener gets it.

• **Organized Pattern.** You remember the song that helps kids learn their ABCs? It's probably been years since you sang or heard it, but you could still sing it. Why? Because of the organized pattern. Try a similar approach with information you want to share and you'll have a great success with the audience remembering it.

• **Identification.** The things we remember best are those that meet our needs the most. When people are able to identify with the information, either emotionally or intellectually, they'll be a lot more apt to remember it.

• **Uniqueness.** When something is unique it stands out. When something stands out, it gives the mind something unusual to tag it to. The result is that it will fare better on the memory curve.

- **Sensory Input.** Everything we experience comes to us through our senses. We remember how something smelled, how it felt to the touch, what it looked like. The more senses you can involve, the more your audience will be able to remember your message.

- **Similar Situation.** Studies have shown that people are more apt to remember something if they are able to re-experience the situation they experienced in the first place. For instance, a witness who's taken back to the scene of the crime will remember more than he will simply sitting in the courtroom. Communicators can use this principle by making sure their messages are placed in a setting that the receiver can easily re-experience.

- **Starting and Ending.** People will remember the beginning and conclusion of a message or experience more than they will the middle. The part remembered most is the ending—put the critical part of your message there.

Memory is always changing and evolving. It is dynamic, not static. The effective communicator is ever looking for ways to increase the information an audience remembers.

The Memory Curve

Percent of Memory Forgotten

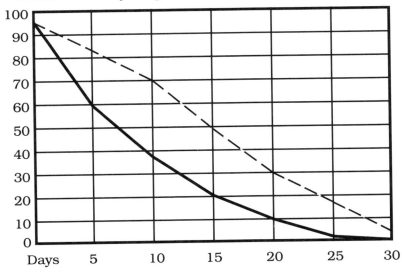

Your objective:
to increase what the audience
remember.

Don't Forget This Element

The receiver is affected by the surroundings.

Communication is always affected by its surroundings. For example, how this book will be received by you, the reader, will depend on:

the lighting as you read it

how hungry you are

your present problems

the temperature in the room

the weather outside

how noisy the room is

how formally or informally you're dressed

the chair you are sitting in

the color of the room

next week's visit by your mother-in-law

how good your eyesight is

In every case it's the same book. But it is perceived differently according to the setting in which the person reads it.

The Cold and Greasy, Plaid and Paisley Talk

Suppose you go to a luncheon. The chicken is cold and greasy, putting you in an awful mood. Then the after-dinner speaker stands up. He's wearing a mixture of plaid and paisley. Somehow it all comes together; you just can't take it anymore. The setting overwhelms you; it overwhelms the message the speaker has. It doesn't matter how good the speech is, you aren't going to hear it.

We often think of setting as purely a physical thing. That's only half right. Also making up the setting are the emotional, cultural, intellectual, political, situational, social, and economical surroundings of the communication. All must be taken into account.

When you put blue with orange, both colors are affected. Both appear deeper and richer than they do alone. The setting has very definitely influenced the communication of each color.

A Set-Up Setting

Two politicians were having a debate. The first speaker understood the value of setting, and before his opponent had a chance to speak, the first politician said, "There's something you should know about my opponent. He'll say or do anything to get elected."

In just a few words, the politician created a bad setting for his opponent. It became a tremendous obstacle that was very difficult to overcome.

When General Motors went overseas, they took their slogan with them: "Body by Fisher." Unfortunately, even though the translation repeated the words faithfully, the new setting (cultural) gave the words a different meaning: "Corpse by Fisher."

Pepsi suffered a similar fate. They moved with their "Come Alive with Pepsi" into the Orient. But they failed to consider the setting. The Orientals read the words as "Pepsi Brings Your Ancestors Back from the Grave."

A major U.S. university once made an embarrassing error because the officials failed to consider a change in setting. The problem came when the administration printed a map of the campus. One building on campus was named the Smith Office Building, in honor of one of the founders. So far, so good.

But then the context changed. The names of all the buildings were abbreviated on the campus maps. And—you guessed it—the Smith Office Building became the SOB.

They saw the error after all the maps were printed.

A change of setting can change the meaning of the communication.

Reduce, Then Rebuild

To improve communication, reduce the information to its simple and general concepts, then rebuild it in concrete terms to match your specific audience.

A Lonely Bird

Here is a description of how one very professional communicator used the approach of reducing and then rebuilding.

One communication problem I was faced with was to tell the story of the Sand Hill Crane at a bird refuge visitors' center. The prime thing to tell was that the Sand Hill Crane was in serious danger of becoming extinct.

How do you communicate "becoming extinct?" I tried to define how that idea made me feel—and the best description I came up with was lonely.

My next step was to search the various media I had available for comparable analogies to loneliness. How do you portray loneliness in color? The answer

was through gray or black. What is the sound of loneliness? A single low note followed by silence. What is spatial loneliness? A single person in an empty room.

I continued my research until I had learned how to communicate loneliness—which equated emotionally to extinction—through all the media I had available to use in the display.

By first reducing the communication problem to a simple concept—loneliness—and then building upon that concept, we arrived at a good solution.

The final exhibit was a small room near the main exhibits at the bird refuge. The doorway to the room was narrowed so that people had to enter one at a time, single file. The carpet on the floor was removed, exposing a hard tile surface that echoed. The room was painted black and gray. The only light in the room was a spotlight trained on the room's only object—a single mounted bird on a pedestal. A recorded message presented the lone cry of a crane surrounded by the low moan of a winter wind. Then in a deep voice, the narrator on the recording briefly told of the Sand Hill Crane's fight for survival and of mankind's responsibility to protect living things.

The Sand Hill Crane exhibit successfully communicated the desired message because we first stripped things back to the most basic level and then built from there. We had to simplify before we could build our complex communication plan.

To effectively comprehend and communicate an idea, one must first isolate that idea; then determine its inherent or natural structure; then restructure that idea to control its perception by an audience.

W.A. Mambert

Relating to Your Audience

What is the age of the earth? The experts disagree, of course—but most are willing to round it off to about five billion years.

Then comes the next question: What in the world is five billion years? It's a number that's next to impossible to relate to. Our span of life is so short; the span of recorded history is but a snap of the fingers compared to the eons that passed before.

The only way to visualize five billion is to create a scale for it. By scaling what you don't know to what you do know, you gain a better understanding of the unknown.

The more new information is scaled or related to previously understood information, the more understandable it will become.

Scale is simply a means of comparison. Scale means comparing a known to an unknown. For example, if you draw a rectangle, those who see it won't have a clue as to the size it represents. So place something known next to it—such as a human. That will give it scale and then the viewer can compare the two, something unfamiliar with something familiar, and know the size you are trying to communicate.

How Much Is a Billion?

Christ was born less than a billion minutes ago. If you wanted to count to a billion, it would take you from birth to retirement at age 65 to accomplish your task. If you took a billion one-dollar bills and stacked them on top of each other, you'd have a pile 69 stories high when you were finished. You'd have to find a pretty tall crane to stack them with!

Consider five billion years as a 20-mile drive:

16 miles—first life on earth

Last 40 feet—the birth of mankind on earth

Last 20th of an inch—formation of the United States

Last 100th of an inch—1990s

If you tried to place a billion dollar bills end to end around the world, they would reach all the way—four times! But over a billion dollars were spent yesterday by the federal government.

Examples of Scale

Look at how you can use the scale of the earth to one man: there are as many living organisms (fungus, germs, bacteria, etc.) on the skin of one man as there are people living on the surface of the earth. The size relationship of a virus to a man is the same as a man to the earth.

Two effective examples of scale: A virus is the same size compared to a man as a man is to the earth.

Scale is an important communication technique. Whenever you want to communicate an idea or fact that is unfamiliar to your audience, think of scale. Compare the unknown to the known, and their range of understanding will increase.

Comparison of a deer to an elk to a moose to a man.

Scale gives understanding by comparison.

How to Get Others to Believe You

If you say there are 300 billion stars in the universe, everyone believes you. But if you say a bench has just been painted, they have to touch it to be sure.

Being believed is as important as being understood.

Believability is as important as the content of the message. You could have the best information on earth, some that is absolutely critical for your audience's survival, but if they won't believe it, the communication will be a waste of breath. Information that isn't believed is never acted upon—and the very purpose of communication is to cause some action.

All Hot or All Wet

You are in a theater and yell, "Fire!" What do the people in the theater do? It all depends on whether or not (and to what degree) they believe what you are yelling.

If you are considered the town prankster, they will probably threaten you and yell back, "Get out of here, you clown!"

If someone considers your yelling a dangerous prank, you may end up meeting the local police officer.

If the people aren't sure whether to believe you or not, they may burn while trying to determine the truth.

If there is a whiff of smoke in the air, your credibility will soar—especially if you have a uniform on.

If one person believes you and starts to run for the exit, his action may cause others to believe. Then look out! There may be a stampede.

Whatever the reaction, it all depends on one thing: how much they believe you.

You Had Better Believe It

Believability goes beyond understanding. Certainly people must get the message before they act. But if they don't believe, they won't change. There will be no action.

Think of when you see special effects in a movie. If you don't "believe" what the movie producer has created, the special effects won't have much of an affect on you. But if he

119

has done a good enough job, you'll drop your disbelief and really become involved. You then step into the screen and become part of the point—the point of believability—at which the movie really starts to be effective. Your heart starts to beat a little faster. Your eyes widen. You may laugh loudly or actually cry—all from something that is fake but still believable.

Believing Factors

Are there ways to increase your chances of being believed? Yes. Here are some things that can help:

- **Identifying yourself with someone or something that is already believed.**

  Walter Cronkite
  Albert Schweitzer
  Mahatma Gandhi
  Red Cross
  the right kind of uniform

- **Surveys have shown who is believed and who is not. For instance, the media trusted most by Americans:**

  television—50 percent
  newspapers—22 percent
  magazines—9 percent
  radio—7 percent

- **People in various careers are trusted as follows:**

  clergy—62 percent
  medical doctors—51 percent
  college teachers—43 percent
  police—37 percent
  lawyers—26 percent
  undertakers—26 percent
  businessmen and executives—15 percent

- **Having someone similar to your audience recommend or witness the truth of what you are saying.**

A mail order firm tested two mailings, one with testimonials and one without. The one with the testimonial did much better than the other—because it was believed more.

The strongest recommendation of all comes from family and friends. Insurance salesmen use this principle when they try to get referrals before they make visits.

- **Letting your audience try or test your communication—and find out that it is true.**

  Seeing is believing for yourself. A free sample will work wonders if you are advocating action. Get the audience to try it on the spot, and they will convince themselves that you should be believed.

- **Showing the audience a similar situation that brought positive results.**

  Commercials that show an imaginary world have long since lost their audiences. But commercials that take a unique approach to showing the product or idea working in the real world are almost always effective.

  One man was trying to sell a water project to a group of people. He told them it would bring great benefits to the area. They were skeptical. But then he showed them some documentation that a similar water project in a similar area had brought the results he was talking about. Instant believability.

- **Stressing the positive effect of your communication.**

  Hope springs eternal in the human soul. People want to believe in something that sounds like it will benefit them. Salvation, wealth, and eternal youth are successfully preached around the world because people want to believe in them.

120

Show that your ideas or product can bring real benefits to the audience and they will believe you because they want it to be true.

• **Giving an impression of personal power.**

The more power you seem to have, the more people will believe you. Jesus taught love and peace and many people turned away. But when he showed mystical power by performing miracles, the people flocked back to him.

Power can also manifest itself in negative ways. Hitler had a power of persuasion—and that power increased as his real power over armies and economies increased.

• **Stressing the negative results they will suffer if they don't listen.**

Just as people want to believe in the hopeful, they know they must believe in the fearful. If they are threatened, they will react by worrying and fighting the threat even if it is only imagined. Probably the most common emotion of all is fear. People fear that their worst fears will come true. They fear they will miss an opportunity. They fear that horrible things will happen to them, or that good things won't happen.

Show them that those fears are probably justified and they will probably believe you more.

Now you know how to be more believable. You can lean back and be smug with me. Because we know the tricks of the trade.

There's only one catch. We'll still believe the next guy who comes along and uses one of these tricks on us!

Being believed is often more important than being understood.

This Rule Has No Exception

This book is full of general principles, methods, and concepts about communication. But it is important to know that **there is an exception to every rule** (except this one). Whenever someone gives you a hard and fast rule, whenever someone says such-and-such won't work, know that someone else has tried such-and-such. And it did work!

For Example

Rule: Small books never make it as best-sellers. And then Richard Bach comes along with Jonathan Livingston Seagull.

Rule: Always seek more understanding of your audience to increase the effectiveness of your communication. But we have seen dozens of examples of the guy who said just what he wanted to say, and the audience could all go lay eggs, for all he cared. And some of those guys are rolling in bucks from the money they're making from their books and seminars.

Whenever there is a communication concept or rule, consider your own situation carefully before you follow it. Communication is a dynamic area. Every situation, every audience, and every subject is unique. General rules are helpful—but only as general rules, not as something set in concrete and reinforced with steel. Your specific communication problem is unique to you.

Be flexible and be smart. Know the rules. But follow them as guides. Don't be their slave. Use them as tools instead.

Evaluating the Audience Profile

How are you going to talk to a group of people unless you know who they are? Suppose you went to a dinner party and were introduced to the "famous Dr. Williams." Great—you start talking shop with him. He stares dumbly at you. Oh-oh. You discover you've got the wrong famous Dr. Williams. You mistook your audience, and in the process the communication failed totally.

Know Your Target

Before you can effectively communicate with anyone, you've got to know who that person is. The more you understand who the audience is, the greater results you can get from your communication.

There are three areas of understanding you should seek about your audience:

Demographic Data will tell you the following about your audience—

    age
    marital status
    number of children

HEIGHT

EDUCATION
SIZE
OCCUPATION
SKILLS

UNIQUE
EXPERIENCES

AGE

SPECIAL
FEATURES

RELIGION
SEX
HEARING
FACIAL FEATURES
EYESIGHT
SPEECH

HABITS
PURCHASE
PREFERENCES
FAMILY
AWARDS

SAVINGS
SICKNESS

TALENTS

INCOME
DONATIONS

ETHNIC
BACKGROUND
TYPE OF HOUSE
CLOTHING
AUTOMOBILE
WEIGHT
HOBBIES

DISTINGUISHING
CHARACTERISTICS

HANDICAPS
SPORTS
ACTIVITIES

DAILY SCHEDULE

economic level
level of education
gender
where they live

Are you trying to present high-yield investments to a hobo?

Are you putting photos on the wall at adult eye-level when your audience is a kindergarten class?

Are you giving a lecture on family planning to a recent widow?

Psychographic Data will give you the audience's emotional background—

religious values
political values
passions
emotional maturity
overriding feelings
expectations, cliches
emotional tendencies
pet peeves

Are you talking about increasing the defense budget to a group of liberal Democrats?

Are you talking about increasing the welfare budget to a group of conservative Republicans?

Are you talking about retirement planning to a group of convicted murderers?

Situation Data will tell you what you need to know about the communication situation itself—

time of day
season, room decor
place, acoustics
temperature, ventilation
seating arrangements
weather

length
lighting, positioning
outside distractions

Are you getting a group excited about waterskiing—in the middle of December?

Are you telling the grisly details of the Texas chainsaw murders—as an after dinner speaker?

Are you droning on and on and on—in a hot, stuffy room?

Carefully consider the important facts about the audience.

Understanding First, Communicating Second

You can't communicate things you don't understand.

It's a basic principle: if you can't comprehend what you're talking about, you can't expect someone else to comprehend your message. You simply can't give away something you don't have.

It's like the nudist who vows to give you the very shirt off his back. He doesn't have a shirt to give, but he's certainly willing to let you have it!

You can have good intentions of sharing your ideas with others. But make sure you understand them yourself. If you don't, you really don't have anything to share.

One Hundred to One

In gaining understanding, you will have to suffer with the 100-to-1 rule, which says that it takes 100 units of preparation to get 1 unit of presentation. If you have a 5-minute speech to give, you'll have to prepare for 500 minutes. If you want to write a 500-

If nothing comes in here . . .

. . . only hot air comes out here.

You must have something inside before you can get it out as a communicator.

page book, you will have to research through 5,000 pages of library material. It will take 100 hours of gaining understanding to be able to communicate effectively for 1 hour.

Of course, that doesn't mean a person has to put in all that time in one concentrated effort. Our entire lives can be part of the preparation we are making. The 100 hours of gaining understanding can come through on-the-job experience, with no study at all involved. But if you haven't had any experience, better plan for failure.

Winston Churchill was well known for his speaking abilities. On more than one occasion he was able to deliver a stirring impromptu speech. Yet he went through years of experience and preparation before he ever said a word. And his most powerful speeches were preceded by hours of careful preparation.

Another effective communicator, Paul Dunn, a well-known speaker to youth groups, has a procedure by which he assures himself that he thoroughly understands his material. First he gives his speech to his kids, and they give him feedback. Then he gives the speech to his wife, who also responds. After going through that process, refining his ideas and presentation as he goes, he finally reaches the point where he feels he really understands what he wants to say. Only then will he stand before the audience to deliver his message.

You can't drink from an empty cup, even if it's a big one.

With all thy getting, get understanding.

Proverbs 4:7

Difficulties with a sentence (or any communication) always mean confused thinking. It is not the sentence that needs straightening out, it is the thought behind it.

Old saying among writers

Blessed is the man who, having nothing to say, abstains from giving in words evidence of the fact.

George Elliot

Knowledge is of two kinds: We know a subject ourselves or we know where we can find information about it.

Sam Johnson

How to Construct a Framework

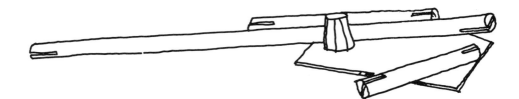

Remember when you used to play with Tinkertoys? You had different kinds of pieces you could fit together. By fitting them in various ways you could make many different things, from boats to windmills to fire engines. But there was always a sequence that worked best. First you'd start with the round piece with holes in it. Then you'd fit it on the support sticks. Then you'd piece together the connecting elements.

The same sequence applies to communication. Before you can build your communication, you need to have a framework. That framework is put together piece by piece. Once you have the framework you can flesh out the details of what you want to say.

Step 1:

Use the round piece. Find the central idea, the key or core point around which everything else will revolve. Keep that central point simple and direct. Everything else will be attached to it, and if you get too complicated the whole structure will be weakened.

Be sure to use only one central piece in your structure. If you get more, the impact of each will be less because of the forced compromise. And the overall impact will be less as well.

To find your central piece, ask these important questions:

What is my purpose?

What do I want as my major thrust?

What are the basic principles I wish to communicate?

What would work as an underlying structure?

Step 2:

Attach the support pieces. Find the elements that support or are subordinate to the central idea and incorporate them into the overall structure.

In taking this step, be sure that you're working toward a unified structure. Consider all the ideas you can and distill out the best. Don't try to keep every little thought you come upon. Remember that you are building only one structure and it should have only one pattern

Just as with your Tinkertoy structure, in your communication structure you need to be able to distinguish the core from the support elements. If you can't, then you need to tear the thing apart and build it again.

Examples of support elements you can include are facts, ideas, figures, symbols, stories, and so forth. Seek to clarify and expand on the core concept, while still remaining true to your original purpose.

Step 3:

Attach connecting pieces. With your core concept in place and the support elements attached, you can now connect your structure into one unified whole. These connecting pieces will make the relationships between each piece obvious. Make sure that your structure at this point is:

a cohesive unit
logically organized
simple
sturdy
relevant
clear
appropriate
accurate

The capability to seek and find order and relationships in ideas, to distinguish between ideas and their parts, between main thoughts and subordinate thoughts, is the root of the capability to effectively isolate, divide, and deal with the ideas you want to handle and communicate.
W.A. Mambert

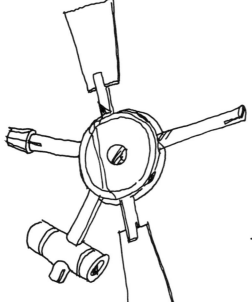

If the structure doesn't fit together well, don't force fit. Find the parts that are causing the trouble and replace them with different ones, or drop them.

The Truth about What People Expect

Expectations are like fences, they often won't let any new ideas in.

For some reason, everyone thinks the world ought to operate according to his or her individual assumptions. One person believes that all car salesmen are crooks. Every experience he has with car salesmen will tend to support his belief. Not because the car salesmen he deals with are really dishonest, but because he simply perceives their actions that way.

Another person may believe that all advertising is a crock. That notion will color the way he receives any advertising he's exposed to. Some of the advertising he sees may actually be quite helpful to him—but he won't perceive it that way, so it won't have that effect.

What people expect to receive from a communication is what they tend to get. To be able to communicate effectively, then, the sender of the message must know what the receiver expects. Once he knows the expectations, he can meet them, putting his message in terms that will match the receiver's anticipations. It is much easier to meet another's expectations than it is to change those expectations.

Reactions According to Expectations

Not too many years ago a new clothes iron was brought onto the market. The designers had decreased the number of holes in the bottom of the iron to decrease the cost. But sales were very low. Why? Because the consumer had a belief that the more holes an iron had, the more effective it was.

That belief wasn't true. But to be able to stay alive, the iron company had to meet the consumers' expectations.

When computers first came on the market they were in huge cabinets. People began to expect them to be a certain size. As years passed, technology shrank the computers smaller and smaller. But some companies found they still had to package them in large cabinets—even though most of the cabinet was almost empty! People expected computers to be huge and wouldn't buy them any other way.

A few days ago a friend of mine went to a movie with his wife. His wife was very excited about the show. She really loved it and raved on and on about it. My friend responded to her expectations and told me how much he liked it. I asked him why. He began to describe the movie to me. "It was great. It was really funny. This happened and this happened." As he talked his enthusiasm waned. He realized what had happened to him: he had let his wife's expectations become his own. At the end of his description he said, "You know, now that I think about it I didn't like that movie at all."

People are rarely so honest with themselves. Generally, they have their present notions, their preconceptions, their expectations, and the communicator must match them or fail.

But in Meeting Them, Great Success Comes

A young couple sat together on a park bench. They snuggled together for a moment, then she asked dreamily, "Do you think my eyes are like stars?"

"Yeah," he answered.

"And do you think my teeth are like pearls?" she continued.

"Yeah, " he said.

"And do you think my hair is like spun gold in the moonlight?"

"Yeah," he repeated.

"Oh, Joe!" she exclaimed ecstatically. "You say the most wonderful things!"

How to Test Your Presentation

A good way to tell if your communication is going to work is to make a model of it and try it out. Make the model as close a representation of the real situation as you can. Put it into a context that is as similar as possible to the planned communication.

The closer you can come to modeling your communication the better the actual communication experience will be.

This idea, model-making, is commonly used:

- Architects make scale models to show their clients what they have in mind.

- Pilots learn how to fly in airplane simulators before they actually go up in the air.

- Film producers create storyboards and scenarios, working out the bugs of the film before they start to make the movie.

- Orators practice in front of a mirror or talk into a tape recorder, giving themselves a dry run before the time for their speech rolls around.

Make a Model of Your Communication

When modeling your communication, do all you can to simulate the setting your communication will take place in. Try to visualize in your mind where the audience will be, how well prepared for your message they will be, how you or your communication vehicle will be situated in relation to the audience, and how the audience will react to your message.

Create your model so you can give it in the context of how the audience will use the information. For instance, a karate school trained its students in all the moves, helping them to know exactly what to do in each situation they might face. But they had the students stop short of actual contact. When the graduates met a real live attacker in the streets, they were unable to hit properly, since they had never experienced contact.

Much better is the example of the swimming school that was training kids to survive falling accidentally into the pool. They threw the kids in—complete with their clothes and

Big Wheels. In that kind of setting the kids were much more able to become "water-proof."

Once you've made the model, test it out. You may find that it is based on assumptions that aren't true or appropriate. Refine your model and evolve it until it's the best you can possibly do, then use it in completing your final communication.

Bibliography

The Art of Plain Talk Rudolf Flesch; Collier Books

Communication Don Fabun; Glencoe Press

Communication Probes Brent D. Peterson et al.; S.R.A.

Effective Communication W.A. Mambert; John Wiley, Inc.

Goal Analysis Robert F. Mager; Fearon-Pitman Publishing

Graphic Design for the Computer Age Edward A. Hamilton; Van Nostrand Reinhold Co.

The Hidden Persuaders Vance Packard; David McKay Company

Instructional Message Design Malcolm Flemingard, W. Howard Levie; Educational Technology Publications

Leadership Effectiveness Training Thomas Gordon; Wyden Books/Bantam Books

Preparing Instructional Objectives Robert F. Mager; Fearon-Pitman Publishing

Rapid Viz Kurt Hanks, Larry Belliston; Crisp Publications, Inc.

The Responsive Chord Tony Schwartz; Anchor Press/Doubleday

Toward a Theory of Instruction Jerome S. Bruner; Harvard

Twenty Questions for the Writer Jacqueline Berke; Harcourt Brace Jovanovich

Understanding Media Marshall McLuhan; McGraw-Hill

Credits

1. Chart by NDEA Project No. 5-16-027, sponsored by the National Art Education Association and the United States Office of Education, printed in Graphic Design for the Computer Age, Edward A. Hamilton, Van Nostrand Reinhold, p. 147.

2. **Symbol Sourcebook**, Henry Dreyfuss, McGraw-Hill.

3. **DRAW! A Visual Approach to Thinking, Learning, and Communicating**, Kurt Hanks and Larry Belliston, Crisp Publications, Inc.

If you have enjoyed this book you will be pleased to learn that CRISP PUBLICATIONS specializes in creative instructional books for both individual and professional growth.

Call or write for our free catalog:

CRISP PUBLICATIONS, INC.
95 First Street
Los Altos, CA 94022

TEL. (415) 949-4888 or
FAX (415) 949-1610

If you have enjoyed this book you will be pleased to learn that CRISP PUBLICATIONS specializes in creative instructional books for both individual and professional growth.

Call or write for our free catalog:

CRISP PUBLICATIONS, INC.
95 First Street
Los Altos, CA 94022

TEL. (415) 949-4888 or
FAX (415) 949-1610